Fernanda Misani v. Ortho Pharmaceutical Corp.
et al. U.S. Supreme Court Transcript of Record
with Supporting Pleadings

Table of Contents

Fernanda Misani v. Ortho Pharmaceutical Corp. et al. U.S. Supreme Court Transcript of Record with Supporting Pleadings

FERNANDA MISANI, CLYDE A SZUCH, Additional Contributors

Fernanda Misani v. Ortho Pharmaceutical Corp. et al.

In The

Supreme Court of the United States

October Term, 1965

No. 595

FERNANDA MISANI,

Plaintiff-Appellant,

v.

ORTHO PHARMACEUTICAL CORPORATION,
a New Jersey corporation, Johnson & Johnson,
a New Jersey corporation, Robert Johnson, Harry
McKenzie, Berton Todd, Evan Spalt, John Friebely,
and William Oroshnik,

Defendants-Respondents,

ON APPEAL FROM THE SUPREME COURT OF NEW JERSEY

JURISDICTIONAL STATEMENT

FERNANDA MISANI,

Plaintiff-Appellant Pro Se,
40 Tamaques Way,
Westfield, New Jersey

Martin Lutz Appellate Printers, Inc.
New York • Philadelphia • Newark • New Brunswick

INDEX

Index

Index

Table of Citations

Page

CASES CITED:

Index

Index

Index

Index

In the

SUPREME COURT OF THE UNITED STATES

October Term 1965

No. _____

Fernanda Misani,

Plaintiff-Appellant,

vs.

Ortho Pharmaceutical Corporation, a New Jersey corporation, Johnson & Johnson, a New Jersey corporation, Robert Johnson, Harry McKenzie, Berton Todd, Evan Spalt, John Friebely, and William Oroshnik,

Defendants-Respondents,

ON APPEAL FROM THE SUPREME COURT OF NEW JERSEY

Jurisdictional Statement

Appellant appeals from the judgment of the Supreme Court of New Jersey dated June 1, 1965 (Appendix A)

which reversed the judgment of the Appellate Division of New Jersey, in favor of the appellant, dated March 11, 1964. The order of the Supreme Court of New Jersey was made final on July 1, 1965, by denial of the petition for rehearing (Appendix A). A notice of appeal was filed with the Clerk of the Supreme Court of New Jersey on August 24, 1965.

Appellant submits this statement to show that the Supreme Court of the United States has jurisdiction of the appeal and that substantial questions are presented.

A. Opinions Below in the First and Second Action.

This is the second action in a nine-year litigation between the same parties. At each stage of the litigation, appellant, plaintiff below, has sought consolidation of the two cases, but it has been denied. The defendants-respondents are Johnson & Johnson, a corporation of New Jersey, Ortho Pharmaceutical Corporation, a totally-owned subsidiary, Robert Johnson, Chairman of the Board, Harry McKenzie, President of Ortho, Berton Todd, Vice-President in charge of Research, Evan Spalt, Vice-President, John Friebely, Director of Personnel, and William Oroshnik, who had an administrative position in the Organic Division.

For the sake of brevity, reference to the respondents will be made hereinafter as "Johnson & Johnson," since the parent company, through a maze of some eighty domestic and foreign subsidiaries, has controlled the business enterprise, and through its legal and patent staff, has directed and handled all phases of the patent matters which are in issue in this case.

a. Opinions below in the first case.

The Trial Court's opinion, dated May 1, 1961, which dismissed plaintiff's case, and the Appellate Division's affirmance, of May 19, 1962, were not published. Petition for certification to the Supreme Court of New Jersey was denied on September 17, 1962. 38 N.J. 304 (1962). Motion for consolidation of the two cases was again denied on December 11, 1962. On April 1, 1963, the United States Supreme Court denied certiorari. 372 U.S. 959 (1963) (Docket No. 819, Fall Term, 1962). Nine copies of that petition with the opinion of the trial court annexed thereto, are submitted together with this Jurisdictional Statement. The disposition of the causes of action in the first case is relevant to determine the extent of res judicata (Question 8 involved in this appeal).

b. Opinions in the second case.

The opinion of the Supreme Court of New Jersey, dated June 1, 1965 is published at 44 N.J. 552; 210 A.2d 609 (1965) and is set forth in Appendix B. The opinion of the Appellate Division, which reversed the trial court and remanded for trial, is published at 83 N.J. Super. 1; 198 A.2d 791 (1964) and is set forth in Appendix C.

B. How the Federal Questions Were Raised.

The constitutional questions involved were properly raised in the trial court, as early as the complaint, and later the pretrial order, request to charge the jury, exception to the Court's charge, argued in all briefs on appeal, Petition for Rehearing, and expressly passed on by the New Jersey courts. After the decision of the Appellate Division in 1964, both parties appealed to the Supreme Court of New Jersey, because of the importance of the federal questions presented.* Since this proceeding draws into question the constitutionality of 35 U.S.C. 101, 102(c), 112, 135, 154, 251, 253 and the applicability of U.S. Constitution, Art. VI, and neither the United States, nor any agency, officer or employee, is a party, it is noted that 28 U.S.C. 2403 may be applicable.

* A certificate of federal questions by the New Jersey Supreme Court has been requested and will be made part of the record as soon as received.

C. Statement of the Grounds on Which the Jurisdiction of this Court is invoked.

(i) The jurisdiction of this Court is founded upon the invalidation of federal law by the New Jersey courts, in a field of federal pre-emption. 28 U.S.C. 1257 (1). In addition, all the questions, including question 8, are sufficiently substantial and important, each in itself, to warrant grant of certiorari. 28 U.S.C. 2103. Briefs and appendixes before the Supreme Court of New Jersey are duly certified and separately presented.

(ii) The texts of the constitutional, statutory provisions, Rules of the United States Patent Office and Excerpts from the Manual of Patent Examining Procedure, U.S. Department of Commerce (1961), involved here, are set forth in Appendix D.

(iii) Appellant is the holder of a degree of Doctor of Philosophy in Organic Chemistry, and an advanced expert in the field of medicinal chemistry (Appendix C, 10a, 25a). In January 1955, she was employed by the respondents with the rank of senior research associate. In April 1956, she was summarily discharged, without notice nor hearing, under the accusation of "incompetency." Johnson & Johnson, Ortho Pharmaceutical Corporation and the individual respondents, circulated, orally and in writing, that her work was no good, deprecated and concealed her inventions, and made it impossible for her to obtain other employment in her field.* The first action was instituted in April 1957 for breach of the contract of employment, fraud at the hiring and defamation. The disposition of the causes of action in

_____

* Appellant has now completed Law School, passed Bar Examinations, and is admitted to practice before the United States Patent Office.

the first case is summarized in Point F (4) of this Jurisdictional Statement, and in the Petition for Certiorari, Docket No. 819, Fall Term, 1962.

During her employment, appellant invented the novel chemical compound "4-methyl 4-phenyl 5-pyrazolone." Three days after the substance had exhibited outstanding value in the treatment of convulsions, she was discharged. In 1959, during the pendency of the first case, respondents secured Letters Patent U.S.P. 2,878,263 which describes in detail the same chemical compound, the novel process of manufacture of the compound and its novel use as a cure against convulsions. The patent designates William Oroshnik, one of the respondents, as inventor. It is shown at page 14, infra.

In 1963, during the pendency of the appeal in this second case, before the Appellate Division of New Jersey, appellant secured, in her name, Letters Patent U.S.P. 3,079,397. Recently, in January 1965, during the pendency of the appeal before the Supreme Court of New Jersey, she secured Letters Patent U.S.P. 3,166,475. The latter issued from a divisional application of the former. The two patents are shown at page 16 and 19, infra. Apart from the technicalities of the language of the claims, the two patents, manifestly, cover the identical subject matter of U.S.P. 2,878,263, which issued in 1959. These two patents, which appellant has obtained in her name, must, under the decisions of the New Jersey courts, now be assigned to Johnson & Johnson. It will be demonstrated infra (page 11) that the two patents were not issued by inadvertence by the United States Patent Office, but with knowledge of the pending litigation and after an interference proceeding with the patent issued in Oroshnik's name.

In September 1959, appellant moved to file a supplemental complaint, in the first case. The motion was denied, on the ground that the two cases were totally different. This second action, instituted in March 1960, sought: 1) an adjudication that respondents had no proprietary rights on the invention, and 2) damages for deprivation of intellectual credit. The complaint alleged wilful and malicious concealment of the invention and fraud on the United States Patent Office for obtaining a patent in the name of one who was not the real inventor.

Trial occurred in April 1962. Appellant's request of a special verdict with written interrogatories to be submitted to the jury, was denied (R213a). The jury rendered a general verdict of no cause of action. On March 11, 1964, the Appellate Division, reversed and remanded the case for trial as to Johnson & Johnson, Ortho and Oroshnik (Appendix C, 41a). On June 1, 1965, the Supreme Court of New Jersey reversed the Appellate Division.

The position of the New Jersey courts on the constitutional questions involved, is:

a) On the matter of ownership, the New Jersey courts compel appellant to assign to Johnson & Johnson her two patents, U.S.P. 3,079,397 and U.S.P. 3,166,475, which issued in 1963 and 1965 respectively, that is, some four and six years after U.S.P. 2,878,263. Appellant's argument that assignment of the two patents violates 35 U.S.C. 154, by rewarding Johnson & Johnson with an extension of the seventeen-year monopoly for the same invention, has been held "frivolous." (Appendix C at 15a; Appendix B at 3a.)

b) On the matter of willful concealment, delay in filing the patent application and deprecation of the invention, during the pendency of the first case, for malicious motives, at a time when respondents wished to represent the appellant as an "incompetent" chemist, the New Jersey courts hold, as a matter of law, that the employer has the absolute right to conceal employees' inventions, even "scrap" them and later seek patent rights (Appendix B at 3a). This holding is repugnant to our constitutional policy, and invalidates 35 U.S.C. 102 (c), as construed by this Court. Electric Battery Co. v. Shimadzu, 307 U.S. 5, 15.

c) With respect to the deprivation of intellectual credit and fraud on the United States Patent Office, the trial judge, after deciding in favor of the employer on the matter of ownership, has held that a scientist, who has agreed to assign proprietary rights to the employer, "forfeits" the right to have his or her name as the inventor, on the patent (R99a; R115a). The Appellate Division reversed (Appendix C, 16a). The Supreme Court of New Jersey, however, has reinstated the judgment of the trial court and holds that it is proper for an employer to obtain a patent in the name of one employee on subject matter invented by another employee. It relieves Johnson & Johnson of liability merely because "the patent claim (one line) was carefully limited to the compound itself" (Appendix B at 7a). Appellant submits that this holding expressly invalidates 35 U.S.C. 101, 112 and 154.

d) The New Jersey courts have permitted Johnson & Johnson, in an action for deprivation of intellectual credit, to argue that U.S.P. 2,878,263 is invalid and appellant was not deprived of credit for something worthless (Appendix C at 9a, 13a, 15a, 28a; Appendix B, at 5a). Appellant's argument that Johnson & Johnson has retained in full monopoly, has enjoyed the benefit of the patent and is estopped to deny the validity, has been rejected.

e) The New Jersey courts have expressly refused to follow substantive rules of the United States Patent Office in a field of federal pre-emption (Appendix C at 34a). Application of 37 C.F.R. 1.216 (a)(4) (Appendix D) would have excluded the testimony of respondent Oroshnik as to his alleged conception of idea of making the substance and would have entitled appellant to judgment, as a matter of law. Oroshnik had no proof whatsoever that he conceived the idea of making the compound, no exhibits and no witnesses. Appellant's testimony, on the other hand, was fully corroborated by authentic exhibits. The motion for judgment has been denied.

(iv) Cases sustaining the jurisdiction of this Court are:

Flournoy v. Wiener, 321 U.S. 253.

Bryant v. Zimmerman, 278 U.S. 63.

Anonymous v. Baker, 360 U.S. 287.

Beecher v. Contour Laboratories, 279 U.S. 388.

Sears, Roebuck & Co. v. Stiffel Company, 376 U.S. 225.

United States v. American Bell Telephone Co., 128 U.S. 315.

Woodbridge v. United States, 263 U.S. 50.

Dalzell v. Dueber Watch Case Manufacturing Co., 149 U.S. 315.

United States v. Dubilier Condenser Corp., 289 U.S. 178.

Sperry v. Florida, 373 U.S. 379.

D. Questions Presented by the Appeal.

The following questions are presented by this appeal:

1. Where the Constitution of the United States (Article I, Sec. 8, Clause 8) grants to Congress the power to promote the progress of science and useful arts, by rewarding authors and inventors with a monopoly "for limited times," and 35 U.S.C. 154 sets the limit at seventeen years, and where the former employer, in 1959, obtained U.S.P. 2,878,263 by fraud on the Patent Office, in the name of one who was not the inventor, and has enjoyed a monopoly under it since 1959, and the Patent Office properly issued in 1963 U.S.P. 3,079,397 and in 1965 U.S.P. 3,166,475 to the real inventor-former employee-appellant here, which cover the identical subject matter of U.S.P. 2,878,263, may the New Jersey courts compel assignment of the two later-issued patents to the former employer, where the net result is to extend the monopoly for the employer beyond the seventeen-year period?

2. May an employer conceal inventions of an employee, and even "scrap" them, as the New Jersey

courts have held, and then, long time afterwards, obtain a patent, deliberately, in the name of one who is not the real inventor?

3. Where a novel process produces a novel product and the product cannot be made by any other process and the product has only one use, in curing a serious disease, do product, process and use constitute a single invention and does the holding of the New Jersey Supreme Court that the claim on the product does not include the process and use, repeal 35 U.S.C. 101, 112 and 154?

4. Where Congress has set up an agency, the Board of Interferences in the United States Patent Office, for the adjudication of inventorship between two contesting parties, and an interference proceeding was instituted, and the Patent Office had no power to compel the patentee to correct certain errors in U.S.P. 2,878,263 to continue the interference, is the holding of the New Jersey courts that the employer-patentee had no duty to correct the errors, repugnant to federal law?

5. Where Congress, by the reissue provisions 35 U.S.C. 251, permits a patentee to correct errors in an issued patent, and the error of U.S.P. 2,878,263 consisted of claiming too broad a monopoly, is the holding of the New Jersey courts that the employer had no duty to narrow the monopoly, repugnant to federal law?

6. Where Congress has enacted the disclaimer provisions, 35 U.S.C. 253, is the employer-patentee, who has continued to assert the full monopoly under U.S.P. 2,878,263, estopped from asserting its invalidity?

7. Does the holding of the New Jersey courts that they are not bound by the rules of the United States Patent Office, violate the Supremacy Clause, U.S. Const., Art. VI?

8. Is the contract as presently enforced against appellant, unconstitutional, and does the application of the doctrine of res judicata in this second case, constitute denial of due process of law?

E. Statement of the Case: The Proceeding in the United States Patent Office.

In December 1959, within one year from the issuance of the patent in Oroshnik's name, as provided by U.S.C. 135, appellant filed a patent application in her name and requested the institution of an interference proceeding with U.S.P. 2,878,263. In compliance with the rule of the United States Patent Office, 37 C.F.R. 1.205, (Appendix D) which controls interferences between an application and an issued patent, she copied the single claim, the broad product claim of U.S.P. 2,878,263, as worded. In addition, she included in her application, narrower claims, covering the novel process of manufacture of the substance and the novel use, as an anticonvulsant.

On May 5, 1960, the United States Patent Office instituted the interference and pursuant to the provision of Manual of Patent Examining Procedure, U.S. Department of Commerce (1961) Sec. 1102.01(b) (Appendix D), notified appellant that, should she lose in the contest with respect to the product claim in issue, the remaining claims in her application would be rejected. The reason was that they were "unpatentable over" the product claim, because integral with the same invention as the product.

In January 1961, the Patent Office notified the parties that the interference, based on the product claim, as worded, would be dissolved, because it claimed a too broad monopoly. The Examiner had discovered a reference, in Beilstein, which anticipated the name and formula of the compound, "a type formula" (R282a; Appendix C at 13a, 19a) but did not anticipate the compound itself. No one had made the substance, no one knew how to make it, nor, obviously, tested the substance or discovered the novel use as an anticonvulsant. Appellant, in reliance on the reissue provisions, 35 U.S.C. 251, which permit a patentee to correct errors in an issued patent and narrow the scope of the monopoly, moved that Johnson & Johnson substitute a narrower claim on the use of the substance as an anticonvulsant, as described in the specification (R211a). Narrowing the scope of the product claim was essential, at that stage, to continue the interference to an adjudication of inventorship.

Johnson & Johnson, however, took advantage of its patentee status and refused to narrow the monopoly.* The United States Patent Office has no jurisdiction to compel a patentee to correct errors and in June 1961 the interference was dissolved, with no adjudication of inventorship (R210a).

Crucial to the questions involved in this appeal, is that, after the interference proceeding, Johnson & Johnson has continued to enjoy the broad monopoly of the product claim and has not disclaimed the patent, as provided by 35 U.S.C. 253.

---

* The legal staff of Johnson & Johnson has essentially admitted that they would have lost the interference proceeding. Rule of the United States Patent Office, 37 C.F.R. 1.216(a)(4) would have excluded the testimony of respondent Oroshnik as to his alleged conception of idea of making the compound, because totally uncorroborated. This topic is discussed below at p.35 of this Jurisdictional Statement.

After the dissolution of the interference, the United States Patent Office withdrew the earlier rejection of process and use claims, and in due course, issued the two patents, U.S.P. 3,079,397 and U.S.P. 3,166,475, in appellant's name. Manifestly the two patents issued because a conflict of interest had been established between appellant and Johnson & Johnson. 35 U.S.C. 135 (Appendix D) provides for the issuance of a second patent for the same invention to a party other than the first patentee, after an interference proceeding. The two patents would not have issued to Johnson & Johnson, because it would have resulted in an extension of the monopoly, "double patenting." In re Dunbar, 278 F.334 (D.C. Cir. 1922);In re Fischel, 136 F.2d 254, 258 (C.C.P.A. 1943); Application of Hession, 296 F.2d 930, 935 (C.C.P.A. 1961).

The two patents, shown at page 16 and 19, cover the identical subject matter of U.S.P. 2,878,263. The compound, 4-methyl 4-phenyl 5-pyrazolone, can only be manufactured by the novel process which is described in detail in U.S.P. 2,878,263. (Compare U.S.P. 2,878,263, Example 1 in Column 2, with U.S.P. 3,079,397, Column 3, lines 45 et seq., Example 2, and Claim 1). The same use, as an anticonvulsant, is described in U.S.P. 2,878,263 and in U.S.P. 3,166,475, Column 3, line 68 to Column 5, line 27. Product, process and use, in this case, constitute a single invention, the making of a novel substance which has utility as a cure against convulsions.

1

2,878,263

4-METHYL-4-PHENYL-5-PYRAZOLONE

William Oroshnik, Plainfield, N. J., assignor to Ortho Pharmaceutical Corporation, a corporation of New Jersey

No Drawing. Application February 14, 1958
Serial No. 715,210

1 Claim. (Cl. 260—310)

This invention relates to 4-methyl-4-phenyl-5-pyrazolone. The novel compound possesses particular value as an anti-convulsant and is useful in the treatment of epilepsy.

Epilepsy has been defined as a cerebral dysrhythmia which may or may not be accompanied by loss of consciousness and body movements. It is now known that epileptic convulsions are related to the flow of electricity from neurons of the cerebral cortex. The type of chemical reaction which is responsible for these cerebral neuronal discharges is not known, but generally, convulsions and loss of consciousness are characterized by abnormally fast brain waves. When the patient suffers loss of consciousness and convulsions, the seizures are referred to as grand mal, a form of major epilepsy. However, convulsions do not necessarily accompany epilepsy, and in some instances consciousness is not lost. When the patient loses consciousness but convulsions are not observed, the attacks are known as petit mal. A third type of epilepsy has been clinically classified as psychomotor epilepsy.

Many drugs are known which reduce or diminish epileptic seizures in man. In general, those drugs which will act as depressants of nervous transmission are effective for this purpose. The hypnotics, such as barbiturates, are effective in doses sufficient to produce anesthesia. Phenobarbital is one of the better anti-convulsants, but must be administered in hypnotic doses. The related hydantoins and oxazolidinediones have also been found to possess anti-convulsant properties. Such drugs, however, interfere to a greater or lesser extent with the normal activities of the patient.

It is most important, that any drug which is used as an anti-convulsant have very low toxicity since the nature of epilepsy requires that the patient use the drug daily and over a long period of time. The ideal anti-convulsant drug should be non-toxic, well tolerated, long acting, and devoid of sedative effects.

It is an object of this invention to provide a new compound, 4-methyl-4-phenyl-5-pyrazolone, which has a high protective index and is non-toxic in use over a long period of time.

Still another object of this invention is to provide a new compound for use in the treatment of epilepsy.

The present invention is particularly concerned with the compound 4-methyl-4-phenyl-5-pyrazolone having the structure

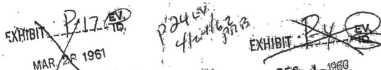

It has been found that the aforesaid compound has unexpected and unobvious properties of great value in combating epilepsy. This compound may take the form of tablets, powders, capsules, or other dosage forms

which will be particularly useful for oral ingestion. The active material, namely the 4-methyl-4-phenyl-5-pyrazolone, may be admixed with solid diluents and/or tableting adjuvants such as corn starch, sucrose, lactose, magnesium stearate, talc, aluminum hydroxide, calcium carbonate; gums such as acacia, or the like. Any of the tableting materials used in pharmaceutical practice may be employed where there is no incompatibility with the 4-methyl-4-phenyl-5-pyrazolone. The material may be placed in a gelatin capsule and administered in that form. Alternatively, the compound may be emulsified in a liquid in which it is not soluble.

Anti-convulsant drugs may be assayed in the laboratory by the minimum electro-shock method. In this procedure, the drug is administered orally to the animals under test. After one hour, the animal is subjected to the direct-current stimulus that is approximately equal to three times the current necessary to produce maximum seizures. The effectiveness of various 3- and 4-substituted-5-pyrazolones as anti-convulsants is summarized in Table I. In this table, the first column gives the effective dose in milligrams per kilogram required to prevent convulsions in one-half of the animals subjected to the minimum electro-shock procedure. The second column indicates the amount of drug in milligrams per kilogram that produced neurological toxic symptoms in one-half of the experimental group. The third column of this table reports the amount of drug, again in milligrams per kilogram, that was fatal to fifty percent of the test group. Column 4 indicates the protective index ($N. T. S._{50} \div ED_{50}$).

TABLE I

	ED_{50}	NTS_{50}	LD_{50}	P.I.
3-undecyl	800+		1,000	
3-dodecyl	800+		1,000	
4-dodecyl	800+		1,000	
4,4-dimethyl	800+		800	
4,4-dibutyl	<1,000	500		
4-phenyl-4-methyl	89	187		2.1

It will be noted that only a single member of the group investigated had a useful protective index.

Example 1

4-METHYL-4-PHENYL-5-PYRAZOLONE

A solution of 4.3 grams (0.021 mole) of ethyl-α-formyl-α-methylphenylacetate, 8.4 milliliters of acetic acid and 3.6 grams of 85% hydrazine hydrate in 300 milliliters of absolute ethanol is refluxed for 14 hours, with condensed ethanol being percolated through a Soxhlet thimble containing 40 grams of calcium oxide before returning to the reaction flask. The alcohol solution is filtered and concentrated under vacuum to a volume of 25 milliliters and diluted with 50 milliliters of water to cause separation of an oily solid which subsequently is leached with 300 milliliters of boiling heptane and filtered. The filtrate is evaporated to 60 milliliters to cause crystallization of a pale yellow solid which subsequently is recrystallized from an acetone-heptane mixture to yield 0.8 gram (22%) of white flakes which melted at 99–101° C. Calcd. for $C_{10}H_{10}N_2O$: N, 16.08. Found N, 15.87.

The percentage of 4-methyl-4-phenyl-5-pyrazolone in compositions for the treatment of epilepsy may be varied. It is necessary that this compound constitute a portion such that suitable dosage will be obtained. The percentage of active agent may be conveniently 10% or 25% or even 50% since activity increases with the concentration of active material. Tablets containing from

2,878,263

3

about 25 to about 50 mg. of 4-methyl-4-phenyl-5-pyrazolone are particularly useful. The following formations are intended to be illustrative only, and may be varied or modified to a considerable extent without departing from the spirit of the invention. We do not therefore intend to limit the invention to the specific embodiments herein set forth.

Example II

	G.
Calcium carbonate	0.500
4-methyl-4-phenyl-5-pyrazolone	0.025
Calcium stearate	0.050

The 4-methyl-4-phenyl-5-pyrazolone is adsorbed onto 10% of the calcium carbonate by mixing. The remaining calcium carbonate, previously granulated with water and dried, is added to this pyrazolone mixture. The calcium stearate is then added and after mixing until uniform, the mixture is compressed into tablets.

4

Example III

	G.
Aluminum hydroxide	0.300
Sucrose	0.100
Lactose	0.100
Gelatin solution	0.005
4-methyl-4-phenyl-5-pyrazolone	0.050
Magnesium stearate	0.005

The 4-methyl-4-phenyl-5-pyrazolone is adsorbed onto 10% of the aluminum hydroxide with mixing. The remainder of the aluminum hydroxide is then granulated with the sucrose, lactose, and gelatin solution and dried at 50° C. These granules are then mixed with the pyrazolone aluminum hydroxide composition and magnesium stearate until uniform and compressed into tablets.

What is claimed is:

The compound 4-methyl-4-phenyl-5-pyrazolone.

No references cited.

United States Patent Office

3,079,397
Patented Feb. 26, 1963

1

3,079,397
PROCESS FOR PREPARATION OF CERTAIN
4,4-DISUBSTITUTED PYRAZOLONES
Fernanda Misani Fiordalisi, 40 Tamaques Way,
Westfield, N.J.
No Drawing. Filed Dec. 29, 1959, Ser. No. 862,450
2 Claims. (Cl. 260—310)

This invention relates to new compounds containing the pyrazolone nucleus and, more particularly, to 4,4-disubstituted 5-pyrazolones.

The pyrazolone nucleus has been known for a long time to exist in three tautomeric structures, and ultra-violet absorption spectra indicate that 1,3-disubstituted 5-pyrazolones may react according to the three following formulae:

Structure I is present in several substituted pyrazolones which are widely known and used as antipyretic agents. Antipyrine, tolypyrine, aminopyrine, melubrine are some of the most important members of this series. All these compounds are characterized by the presence of a phenyl group attached to the nitrogen atom in the 1-position and a methyl group in the 3-position. The 4-position is usually, but not necessarily, substituted, because for instance it is unsubstituted in antipyrine and tolypyrine. The nitrogen atom in the 2-position is substituted in antipyrine and melubrine, but it is unsubstituted in aminopyrine.

It seems reasonable to conclude that a phenyl group in the 1-position and a methyl group in the 3-position are essential for antipyretic activity, but that substitution in the 4-position is not essential.

Several 4,4-dimethyl derivatives, as well as Pyrazole Blue and Tartrazine, are derived from Formula II. The existence of structure III has been invoked to explain the products resulting from methylation with diazomethane or acylation with acid chlorides and alkali, which are O-alkyl and O-acyl derivatives. Several pyrazolone dyes are derived from structure III.

In spite of the extensive research in the field of pyrazolones, no pharmacological or clinical use has ever been reported for any compound derived from structure II, more specifically for compounds containing two substituents in the 4-position. In view of the extensive literature data in the field of pyrazolones and the absence of any physiological activity of the known pyrazolones derived from structure II, it was novel and surprising to find that compounds derived from structure II possess significant value as central depressants and more particularly as anticonvulsants.

The object of this invention is to prepare 4,4-disubstituted pyrazolones, which are unsubstituted on the two nitrogen atoms.

Another object of the invention is to describe the novel method used for the preparation of the compounds of the invention.

Other objects of the invention will appear from the specification and examples.

The compounds of the invention have the formula:

2

in which R is an alkyl group containing up to four carbon atoms, R' is an aryl group and R" is selected from the group consisting of hydrogen and a low-molecular-weight alkyl group. It is also possible, according to the invention, that R and R' represent the same substituent.

In view of the essential features indicated above, exhibited by compounds having antipyretic activity, that is, a phenyl group on the nitrogen in the 1-position and a methyl group in the 3-position, it was also novel and unforeseeable that the anticonvulsant activity reaches the maximum value in 4-methyl-4-phenyl pyrazolone, that is, a compound which is unsubstituted both on the two nitrogen atoms and in the 3-position.

The anticonvulsant activity of the compounds of this invention may perhaps be explained by the fact that they contain the group

$$-\text{NHCOC(RR')}$$

that is, these compounds are structurally related to known hypnotics and central depressants. It is not a mere coincidence that this moiety is found for instance in hydantoins, disubstituted barbiturates, oxazolidinediones, hexahydropyrimidinediones, Neludar and Doriden.

The fact that the two substituents in the 4-position of the pyrazolones of this invention are essential to physiological activity is analogous to the barbiturates where 5-unsubstituted or 5-mono-substituted barbiturates are well known to be devoid of any physiological activity. Although the mechanism of action of the compounds of the invention appears to be analogous to the known central depressants, it is to be understood that the scope of this invention is not limited by theoretical consideration of mode of action on the brain centers, mainly because such a mode of action is still little known or inadequately understood.

Anticonvulsant activity is the ability of a compound to prevent epileptic seizures, that is, convulsions accompanied by loss of consciousness, which are known as "grand mal epilepsy," and also the ability to control the milder attacks not accompanied by convulsions, known as "petit mal."

The method used for the preparation of the compounds of the invention consisted of the reaction of an α,α-disubstituted ester containing a carbonyl group in the β-position with hydrazine, as represented below:

$$R''COC(RR')COOC_2H_5 + NH_2NH_2 \longrightarrow$$

According to this equation, R, R' and R" have the same meaning as indicated above, that is, R and R' may be the same or different and may be either an alkyl group containing up to four carbon atoms or an aryl group, and R" may be hydrogen or a low-molecular-weight alkyl group. It is also possible that R and R' are the same.

The synthesis of the compounds of this invention offered considerable difficulties. In Karrer "Organic Chemistry" (Elsevier Publishing Company), 4th edition (1950), it is stated on page 798:

"A very general synthesis of pyrazolone compounds consists in the action of hydrazine or hydrazine derivatives on esters of β-ketonic acids. If formyl acetic ester is used in place of the latter, the parent substance, the simplest pyrazolone, is formed."

In spite of the statement found in Karrer and in spite of the fact that the literature shows many examples of pyrazolone synthesis from phenylhydrazine and substituted acetoacetic esters, when this basic reaction was applied to the synthesis of the compounds of this invention, using hydrazine and disubstituted β-keto- or β-formyl

3,079,397

3

esters, the reaction was satisfactory only with the lower members of the series. For instance, 3,4,4-trimethyl pyrazolone was satisfactorily prepared from dimethyl acetoacetic ester and hydrazine, but the reaction failed when applied to the dibutyl acetoacetic ester. Essentially, the reaction is an addition of hydrazine to the carbonyl group, complicated by the basic character of hydrazine, which is a stronger base than phenylhydrazine, the lack of enolization in the ester component because the presence of two substituents in the α-position and the relatively higher molecular weight of the two substituents, that is, the butyl groups instead of methyl groups. The lack of enolization in the ester component is responsible for the difficulty in the formation of the ester-hydrazine transition complex, represented below by Formula A

$$R''COC(RR')COOEt + NH_2NH_2 \longrightarrow$$

$$R''\overset{O\ominus}{\underset{\oplus NH_2NH_2}{\overset{|}{C}}}(RR')COOEt \longrightarrow \quad (A)$$

$$R''\overset{OH}{\underset{NHNH_2}{\overset{|}{C}}}(RR')COOEt \overset{-H_2O}{\underset{-EtOH}{\longrightarrow}} \quad (B)$$

The high basicity of hydrazine is expected to make the proton transfer from this transition complex A to the compound shown by B more difficult than in the corresponding complex, where phenylhydrazine is involved. Obviously, the equilibrium is not in favor of the hydrazone formation, and for the pyrazolone synthesis which involves a further cyclodehydration step to give C. The above mentioned theoretical considerations led to the adoption of the following method. It was found that the reaction proceeds satisfactorily by allowing equivalent amounts of hydrazine and the α-disubstituted β-keto or β-formyl ester to react overnight after adjusting the pH to 5, under conditions which provide for the removal of the water formed in the reaction. Thus, decrease of basicity and shifting the equilibrium in favor of the pyrazolone by elimination of the water formed proved very advantageous.

The reaction may be conveniently carried out by placing molar equivalents of hydrazine and of the ester component, preferably in a solvent, in a flask provided with a Soxlet extraction apparatus and placing a dehydrating agent in the thimble of the Soxlet extraction apparatus. Calcium oxide and barium oxide are suitable dehydrating agents, but other dehydrating agents, such as magnesium sulfate and calcium sulfate, may be used. The amount of the dehydrating agent should be sufficient to absorb all the water formed in the reaction, but an excess is preferable.

Obviously, any technique, which allows for the removal of water, is satisfactory, althought the procedure comprising refluxing in a Soxlet apparatus with calcium oxide represents the preferred embodiment of the invention. Ethanol is a suitable solvent, but other solvents inert to the reactants may be used.

The method has general application for the synthesis of pyrazolones containing two relatively high-molecular-weight substituents in the 4-position and characterized by the absence of substituents on the two nitrogen atoms.

The following examples are given for the purpose of illustrating the invention, but it is to be understood that the invention is to be limited only by the appended claims.

EXAMPLE 1

3-Methyl-4,4-Dibutyl-Pyrazolone

5 g. of ethyl dibutyl aceto-acetate, 3.4 g. of 85% hydrazine hydrate were dissolved in 150 ml. ethanol and the pH was adjusted to about 5 by dropwise addition of acetic acid. The solution was refluxed for about 16 hours

4

in a flask provided with a Soxlet thimble containing 20 g. of calcium oxide. Then the solution was filtered to remove traces of calcium oxide carried over into the flask, concentrated to about 15 ml. and diluted with an equal volume of water. A crop of 3 g. of product having a melting point of 95–100° C. was obtained, which was further purified by recrystallization from benzene and precipitation with petroleum ether (B.P. 70–90° C.). The melting point of the pure product was 102–103° C. *Analysis.*—Calcd. for $C_{12}H_{22}N_2O$: C, 68.53; H, 10.54. Found: C, 68.69; H, 10.62.

The substance showed some anticonvulsant activity, but was more toxic than the 4-phenyl-4-methyl compound described in Example 2.

EXAMPLE 2

4-Methyl-4-Phenyl-5-Pyrazolone

Four and three tenths of a gram of ethyl α-formyl α-methyl phenyl acetate, 3.6 grams of 85% hydrazine hydrate were dissolved in 300 ml. of absolute ethanol, and the solution was brought to pH 5 by dropwise addition of acetic acid. The solution was placed in a flask provided with a Soxlet apparatus, and 40 grams of calcium oxide were placed in the thimble. After refluxing for about 17 hours, the solution was filtered, concentrated to about 25 ml. and diluted with an equal volume of water. The crude product, 2.3 grams, recrystallized from heptane and acetone, gave a crop of 1.6 grams of melting point 98–101° C.

Extraction with heptane and concentration of the heptane solution raised the melting point to 99–101° C. *Analysis.*—Calcd. for $C_{10}H_{10}N_2O$: N, 16.08. Found: N, 15.87.

4-methyl-4-phenyl pyrazolone was tested by the minimum electro-shock procedure. The animals were administered the substance orally, and after one hour they were subjected to the direct crurent stimulus, that is, to about three times the current necessary to produce maximum seizures. The dose required to prevent convulsions in one half of the animals tested, in milligrams per kilogram, that is ED_{50}, was 89. The substance had low toxicity, because the NTS_{50}, that is the amount of drug in milligrams per kilogram, which produced neurological toxic symptoms in one half of the animals tested, was 187.

The 3-methyl-4,4-dibutyl pyrazolone, prepared according to Example 1, showed some anticonvulsant activity, but was less active than 4-methyl-4-phenyl-pyrazolone, and more toxic.

It appears that the absence of the methyl group in position 3 and the presence of a phenyl group in position 4 are beneficial for anticonvulsant activity.

I claim;

1. The process of preparing 4,4-disubstituted pyrazolones of formula

wherein each of R and R^1 is a member selected from the group consisting of alkyl of 1 to 4 carbon atoms and phenyl, further characterized by the fact that R may be the same as R^1, and R^{11} is a member selected from the group consisting of hydrogen and lower alkyl, which comprises the steps of adjusting to about 5 the pH of an ethanolic solution of a compound of formula $R^{11}COC$-$(RR^1)COOR^{111}$, wherein R, R^1 and R^{11} have the same meaning as above and R^{111}, is lower alkyl, and the equivalent amount of hydrazine hydrate, refluxing said solution in a flask provided with a Soxlet thimble, said thimble containing a dehydrating agent which is a member selected from the group consisting of CaO, BaO, $MgSO_4$, Na_2SO_4 and anhydrous K_2CO_3, continuing refluxing until all the water formed is removed, and isolating said 4,4-disubstituted pyrazolone from the reaction mixture.

3,079,397

5

2. The process according to claim 1, wherein said dehydrating agent is CaO in amount exceeding the theoretical amount required to remove the water formed in the reaction.

References Cited in the file of this patent

UNITED STATES PATENTS

2,637,732	Schmid et al.	May 5, 1953
2,878,263	Oroshnik	Mar. 17, 1959
2,933,391	Feniak et al.	Apr. 19, 1960

6

OTHER REFERENCES

Backer et al.: Chem. Abstracts, volume 20, page 1990 (1926).

Beilstein (Handbuch, 4th edition), volume 24, 2nd Supplement, page 80 (1954).

Veibel et al.: Chem. Abstracts, volume 49, column 14741 (1955).

Elderfield: "Heterocyclic Comp'ds," volume 5, pages 114–119 (1957).

United States Patent Office

3,166,475
Patented Jan. 19, 1965

1

3,166,475
ANTI-CONVULSANT PYRAZOLONES
Fernanda Misani Fiordalisi, 40 Tamaques Way,
Westfield, N.J.
No Drawing. Original application Dec. 29, 1959, Ser.
No. 862,450, now Patent No. 3,079,397, dated Feb. 27,
1963. Divided and this application Dec. 31, 1962,
Ser. No. 248,216
6 Claims. (Cl. 167—65)

This is a division of application Serial No. 862,450,
filed December 29, 1959, now U.S. Patent No. 3,079,397.

This invention relates to a method for relieving convulsions and is more particularly concerned with a method for relieving convulsions in animals.

The invention is based on the unexpected finding that certain 4-4-disubstituted pyrazolone compounds, when administered to the animal organism, exhibit anti-convulsant activity.

The pyrazolone nucleus has been known for a long time to exist in three tautomeric structures, and ultraviolet absorption spectra indicate that 1,3-disubstituted 5-pyrazolones may react according to the three following formulae:

I   II   III

Structure I is present in several substituted pyrazolones which are widely known and used as antipyretic agents. Antipyrine, tolypyrine, aminopyrine, melubrine are some of the most important members of this series. All these compounds are characterized by the presence of a phenyl group attached to the nitrogen atom in the 1-position and a methyl group in the 3-position. The 4-position is usually, but not necessarily, substituted, because for instance it is unsubstituted in antipyrine and tolypyrine. The nitrogen atom in the 2-position is substituted in antipyrine and melubrine, but it is unsubstituted in aminopyrine. Thus while the phenyl group in the 1-position and a methyl group in the 3-position seem to be essential for antipyretic activity, substitution in the 4-position does not appear to be essential.

Several 4,4-dimethyl derivatives, as well as Pyrazole Blue and Tartrazine, are derived from Formula II. The existence of structure III has been invoked to explain the products resulting from methylation with diazomethane or acylation with acid chlorides and alkali, which are C-alkyl and O-aryl derivatives. Several pyrazolone dyes are derived from Structure III.

In spite of the extensive research in the field of pyrazolones no pharmacological or clinical use has ever been reported for any compound derived from structure II, more specifically for compounds containing two substituents in the 4-position. In view of the extensive literature data in the field of pyrazolones and the absence of any physiological activity of the known pyrazolones derived from structure II, it was novel and surprising to find that compounds derived from structure II possess significant value as central depressants and more particularly as anti-convulsants.

The compounds of the invention have the formula:

2

in which R is an alkyl group containing up to four carbon atoms, R' is an aryl group and R'' is selected from the group consisting of hydrogen and a low-molecular-weight alkyl group. It is also possible, according to the invention, that R and R' represent the same substituent.

In view of the essential features indicated above, exhibited by compounds having antipyretic activity, that is, a phenyl group on the nitrogen in the 1-position and a methyl group in the 3-position, it was also novel and unforeseeable that the anti-convulsant activity reaches the maximum value in 4-methyl-4-phenyl pyrazolone, that is, a compound which is unsubstituted both on the two nitrogen atoms and in the 3-position.

The anti-convulsant activity of the compounds of this invention may perhaps be explained by the fact that they contain the group

$$-NHCOC(RR')$$

that is, these compounds are structurally related to known hypnotics and central depressants. It is not a mere coincidence that this moiety is found for instance in hydantoins, disubstituted barbiturates, oxazolidinediones, hexahydropyrimidinediones, Noludar and Doriden.

The fact that the two substituents in the 4-position of the pyrazolones of this invention are essential to physiological activity is analogous to the barbiturates where 5-unsubstituted or 5-monosubstituted barbiturates are well known to be devoid of any physiological activity. Although the mechanism of action of the compounds of the invention appears to be analogous to the known central depressants, it is to be understood that the scope of this invention is not limited by theoretical consideration of mode of action on the brain centers, mainly because such a mode of action is still little known or inadequately understood.

Anticonvulsant activity is the ability of a compound to prevent epileptic seizures, that is, convulsions accompanied by loss of consciousness, which are known as "grand mal epilepsy," and also the ability to control the milder attacks not accompanied by convulsions, known as "petit mal."

The process used for the preparation of the compounds of the invention has been described in copending application Serial No. 862,450, filed December 29, 1959, now issued to U.S.P. 3,079,397. The process consisted of the reaction of an α,α-disubstituted ester containing a carbonyl group in the β-position with hydrazine, as represented below:

$$R''COC(RR')COOC_2H_5 + NH_2NH_2 \longrightarrow$$

According to this equation, R, R' and R'' have the same meaning as indicated above, that is, R and R' may be the same or may be different and may be either an alkyl group containing up to four carbon atoms or an aryl group, and R'' may be hydrogen or a low-molecular-weight alkyl group. R and R' may also be the same.

The process described and claimed in Serial No. 862,-450 essentially consists of placing molar equivalents of hydrazine and of the ester component, preferably in a solvent, in a flask provided with a Soxhlet extraction apparatus adjusting the pH to 5, and placing a dehydrating agent in the thimble of the Soxhlet extraction apparatus. Calcium oxide and barium oxide are suitable dehydrating agents, but other dehydrating agents, such as magnesium sulfate and calcium sulfate, may be used. The amount of the dehydrating agent should be sufficient to absorb all

3,166,475

3

the water formed in the reaction, but an excess is preferable.

Obviously, any technique, which allows for the removal of water, is satisfactory, although the procedure comprising refluxing in a Soxhlet apparatus with calcium oxide represents the preferred embodiment of the invention. Ethanol is a suitable solvent, but other solvents inert to the reactants may be used.

The method has general application for the synthesis of pyrazolones containing two relatively high-molecular-weight substituents in the 4-position and characterized by the absence of substituents on the two nitrogen atoms.

The following preparations and examples are meant to be illustrative of the process and products of the present invention and are not to be construed as limiting.

PREPARATION I

3-methyl-4,4-dibutyl-pyrazolone.—5 g. of ethyl dibutyl aceto-acetate, 3.4 g. of 35% hydrazine hydrate were dissolved in 150 ml. ethanol and the pH was adjusted to about 5 by dropwise addition of acetic acid. The solution was refluxed for about 16 hours in a flask provided with a Soxhlet thimble containing 20 g. of calcium oxide. Then the solution was filtered to remove traces of calcium oxide carried over into the flask, concentrated to about 15 ml. and diluted with an equal volume of water. A crop of 3 g. of product having a melting point of 95- recrystallization from benzene and precipitation with 100° C. was obtained, which was further purified by petroleum ether (B.P. 70-90° C.). The melting point of the pure product was 102-103° C. *Analysis.*—Calcd. for $C_{12}H_{22}N_2O$: C, 68.53; H, 10.54. Found: C, 68.69; H, 10.62.

The substance showed some anti-convulsant activity, but was more toxic than the 4-phenyl-4-methyl compound described below.

PREPARATION II

4-methyl-4-phenyl-5-pyrazolone.—Four and three-tenths of a gram of ethyl α-formyl α-methyl phenyl acetate, 3.6 grams of 85% hydrazine hydrate were dissolved in 300 ml. of absolute ethanol, and the solution was brought to pH 5 by dropwise addition of acetic acid. The solution was placed in a flask provided with a Soxhlet apparatus, and 40 grams of calcium oxide were placed in the thimble. After refluxing for about 17 hours, the solution was filtered, concentrated to about 25 ml. and diluted with an equal volume of water. The crude product, 2.3 grams, recrystallized from heptane and acetone, gave a crop of 1.6 grams of melting point 98-101° C.

Extraction with heptane and concentration of the heptane solution raised the melting point to 99-101° C. *Analysis.*—Calcd. for $C_{10}H_{10}N_2O$: N, 16.08. Found: N, 15.87.

PREPARATION III

4,4-dimethyl pyrazolone.—The substance was prepared by heating 4 hours equivalent amounts of hydrazine hydrate and ethyl α-formyl isobutyrate. After cooling, the product was extracted with ether and recrystallized from benzene petroleum ether—M.P. 97°-98°.

Experiment 1.—Acute toxicity—mice

The test compounds in 1.5 to 2% solution were administered intraperitoneally in graded doses to a group of mice and the number of deaths recorded. The dose which should kill 50 percent of the animals, that is the LD_{50}, was calculated. The results are summarized below.

Test compound:	LD_{50}, mg./kg.
4,4-dimethyl pyrazolone	>900
3-methyl-4,4-dibutyl-pyrazolone	400
4-methyl-4-phenyl pyrazolone	1000

Experiment 2.—Neurological toxic symptoms

The procedure was essentially the same as in the previous experiment, except that instead of death, the end

4

point was the development of neurological toxic symptoms in one-half of the experimental group of mice.

Test compounds:	NTD_{50} in mg./kg.
4,4-dimethyl pyrazolone.	
3-methyl-4,4-dibutyl pyrazolone	500
4-methyl-4-phenyl pyrazolone	187

Experiment 3.—Anticonvulsant

A. The test procedure was the electroshock method, that is the drug was administered orally to the mice under test. After one hour the animal was subjected to the direct-current stimulus, about equal to three times the current necessary to produce maximum seizures. The results below give the effective dose in milligrams per kilogram required to prevent convulsions in one-half of the animals tested.

Test compound:	ED_{50} in mg./kg.
4,4-dimethyl-pyrazolone	>800
3-methyl-4,4-dibutyl pyrazolone	1000
4-methyl-4-phenyl pyrazolone	89

The Protective Index against electroshock of 4-methyl-4-phenyl pyrazolone is

$$\frac{NTD_{50}}{ED_{50}} = \frac{187}{89} = 2.1$$

that is the substance has a high protective index and is essentially non-toxic, as demonstrated by the high doses required to produce neurological toxic symptoms or to kill one-half of the animals under test.

B. Anticonvulsant activity against metrazole:

Test compound:	ED_{50} in mg./kg.
4,4-dimethyl pyrazolone	>800
3-methyl-4,4-dibutyl pyrazolone	750
4-methyl-4-phenyl pyrazolone	116

The 3-methyl-4,4-dibutyl pyrazolone gave no evipal potentiation at 125 mg./kg. A slight evipal potentiation was noticed with 4,4-dimethyl pyrazolone at 800 mg./kg.

The above data show that while the 4,4-dimethyl and the 3-methyl-4,4-dibutyl pyrazolone give no protection at a dose of 800 mg./kg., 4-methyl-4-phenyl pyrazolone has a protective index against metrazole of 1.6.

Experiments 4 and 5.—Analgesic and hypnotic activity

Test compound:	ED_{50}
4,4-dimethyl pyrazolone	>800
3-methyl-4,4-dibutyl pyrazolone	>1000
4-methyl-4-phenyl pyrazolone	>500

These data show that the 4,4-disubstituted pyrazolones in direct contrast with 5,5-disubstituted barbituric acids have no hypnotic nor sedative activity. This property is very significant in the field of anticonvulsants, where it may be necessary to continue the use of the drug over an extended period of time, and it is desirable not to interfere with the normal activities of the patient. The anticonvulsant activity of the 4,4-disubstituted pyrazolones still shows a correlation with the structure of the two substituents in position 4 as the substituents, the activity being negligible in the case of two low-molecular weight substituents, and being highest with 4-methyl-4-phenyl pyrazolone, which is the closest to phenobarbital.

While the compounds of the present invention may be administered to the animal organism intravenously, and intraperitoneally, it is contemplated that the preferred method of administration will be oral. For oral administration, they may be conveniently administered in the form of essentially pure undiluted compounds, such as in a gelatin capsule. Preferably, for ease of handling, the compounds may be intimately associated with a liquid or solid carrier. Sterile water is the preferred liquid carrier, in the presence of an emulsifier. Solid pharmaceutical carriers such as starch, sugar, talc, aluminum hydroxide, calcium carbonate, and the like may be used to form powders. The powders may be tabletted by

3,166,475

5

means of suitable lubricants such as magnesium stearate, or binders such as gelatin.

The compounds may also be converted into their acid addition salts which are prepared from the free bases in a conventional manner by reacting the free bases with the usual inorganic acids, which include for purposes of illustration but without limitation hydrochloric, hydrobromic, hydriodic, sulfuric, and phosphoric or an organic acid, such as formic, methanesulfonic tartaric, citric succinic, et cetera. If the salts are used, the powders may be tabletted with disintegrating agents such as sodium bicarbonate.

The compounds useful as anticonvulsants according to the present invention may be formed in unit dosages containing predetermined amounts of the useful compounds which may then be administered at regular time intervals to create and maintain effective body levels. Suggested unit dosages of 4-methyl-4-phenyl pyrazolone for larger animals are 25 to 50 mgs. of the active compound per tablet or capsule or a solution containing 25 to 50 mgs. of the useful compound per teaspoon. In the formulations, the percentage of 4-methyl-4-phenyl pyrazolone may vary from 10% up to 50%, the remainder being any of the inert ingredients mentioned above or their combinations. This invention can be embodied in other specific forms without departing from its scope which is to be limited only by the appended claims.

I claim:

1. The method of combating convulsions in animals which comprises administering into the animal dosage units of a pharmaceutically acceptable form of a 4,4-disubstituted pyrazolone of formula

wherein each of R and R' is a member selected from the group consisting of lower alkyl containing between 1 and 4 carbons atoms and phenyl, further characterized by the fact that the sum of carbon atoms of R and R' is greater than 4 and that R may be the same as R' when R and R' total at least eight carbon atoms, and R'' is

6

selected from the group consisting of hydrogen and lower alkyl.

2. The method according to claim 1 wherein said pyrazolone is 4-methyl-4-phenyl pyrazolone.

3. The method according to claim 1 wherein said pyrazolone is 3-methyl-4,4-dibutyl pyrazolone.

4. The method of combating convulsions in animals which comprises orally administering into the animal doses of 25 to 50 mgs. of a pharmaceutically acceptable form of 4-methyl-4-phenyl-5-pyrazolone.

5. An anticonvulsant composition comprising between 10 and 50% of an active compound of the formula

wherein each of R and R' is a member selected from the group consisting of lower alkyl containing between 1 and 4 carbon atoms and phenyl, further characterized by the fact that the sum of carbon atoms of R and R' is greater than 4 and that R may be the same as R' when R and R' total at least eight carbon atoms and R'' is selected from the group consisting of hydrogen and lower alkyl, and the remainder is an inert carrier which is a member selected from the group consisting of talc, aluminum hydroxide, sugar, starch, gelatin, magnesium stearate and combinations thereof.

6. The method of treating an animal suffering from convulsive spasm which comprises administering to said animal a therapeutic dose of 4-methyl-4-phenyl-5-pyrazolone, said dose being less than the neurotoxic dose.

References Cited in the file of this patent
UNITED STATES PATENTS

2,878,263   Oroshnik _____ Mar. 17, 1959

OTHER REFERENCES

Beilsteins, vol. 24, 2nd Supp., p. 80, 1954.

JULIAN S. LEVITT, *Primary Examiner.*

FRANK CACCIAPAGLIA, Jr., LEWIS GOTTS,
Examiners.

F. The Questions Presented are Substantial.

(1) Patent Misuse: Extension of the Monopoly.

Our patent laws are designed to promote the progress of science and useful arts by encouraging inventors to make their inventions known rather than to keep them secret. The contract between the inventor and the public is a monopoly for seventeen years, in return for the dedication to the public of the know-how and a full description of the manner of carrying out and using the invention. 35 U.S.C. 112; Coffin v. Ogden, 18 Wall. (85 U.S.) 120; Application of Schlittler, 234 F.2d 882 (C.C.P.A. 1956). On the date of the issuance of the patent, the patentee acquires the exclusive right to make, use and sell his invention, in accordance with the details described in the specification. 35 U.S.C. 154.

Question 1 in this case involves patent misuse as defined by this Court. Any legal device employed by the inventor, or anyone claiming under him, to secure, to any extent, an extension of his monopoly, is a patent misuse and runs counter to the policy of our patent laws. The doctrine is founded on reasons of public policy. Scott Paper Co. v. Marcalus Mfg. Co., 326 U.S. 249, 256; Mercoid Corp. v. Mid-Continent Invest. Co., 320 U.S. 661, 665; Ethyl Gasoline Corporation v. United States, 309 U.S. 436; Sears, Roebuck & Co. v. Stiffel Co., 376 U.S. 225, 229; Brulotte v. Thys, 379 U.S. 29.

Appellant has urged that if U.S.P. 3,079,397 and U.S.P. 3,166,475 which cover the identical subject matter of U.S.P. 2,878,263, are assigned to Johnson & Johnson, the effect will be an unconstitutional extension of the seventeen-year monopoly. The New Jersey Supreme Court disposes of the issue with the holding that "the patent claim in [U.S.P. 2,878,263] was carefully limited to the compound itself and did not extend to the process and use." (Appendix B at 7a). Appellant submits that this holding is replete with errors and invalidates 35 U.S.C. 101, 112 and 154. A claim must be read in the light of the specification, a copy of which is annexed and made part of the Letters Patent. 35 U.S.C. 154.

By the express statutory language, 35 U.S.C. 154, the patent claim on the compound itself in U.S.P. 2,878,263, gave Johnson & Johnson the right of making, using and selling the compound, by reference to the specification for the details. Obviously Johnson & Johnson in 1959 acquired the right to make the substance, by the novel process and for the use described in the specification. In this case, the novel process for making the product and the novel use of the substance, are integral with the invention for the product. The substance cannot be made except by the process described in the specification and has no other utility except as described therein. (Appendix C, at 21a.) The invention, stripped of the technicalities of the language of the claims, resides in the making of a novel substance, 4-methyl 4-phenyl 5-pyrazolone, which shows novel non-obvious utility to treat convulsions.

In James v. Campbell, 104 U.S. 356, 377, 382, this Court said:

> "Where a new process produces a new substance, the invention of the process is the same as the invention of the substance...It is hardly necessary to remark that the patentee could not include in a subsequent patent any invention embraced or described in a prior one."

In Miller v. Eagle Manufacturing Co., 151 U.S. 186, 198, a distinction was made between the same patentee and another party:

> "...no patent can issue for an invention actually covered by a former patent especially to the same patentee, although the term of the claims may differ..." (Emphasis added.)

Accord, Mosler Safe Co. v. Mosler, 127 U.S. 354, 361. One Court has paraphrased the same rule by stating that a patentee may not extract an essential element from his own prior patent, without which the former patent would not have been granted, and make it the subject of a subsequent patent. Palmer Pneumatic Tire Co. v. Lozier, 90 Fed. 732 (6th Cir. 1898). It would amount to "double patenting."

In determining whether a second patent is distinct from the earlier one, courts do not consider merely a one-line claim, but whether the specifications are substantially different and whether the claims of the later patent find support in the earlier patent. Miller v. Eagle Manufacturing Co., supra, at 202. U.S.P. 2,878,263, involved in this appeal, would not have issued, without a full description of the process and use of the product. Further, the two later patents, in appellant's name, U.S.P. 3,079,397 and U.S.P. 3,166,475, add nothing to the state of the art. The claims find complete support in the specification of the earlier patent. The only exception to the seventeen-year monopoly, for the same invention, is permitted where there is a conflict of interest, in the case of an interference, as in this instant case, and the subsequent patent is awarded to the real inventor, a party other than the first patentee. 35 U.S.C. 135. The United States Patent Office would not have issued the two later patents to Johnson & Johnson.

There may be instances in which product, process and use are separable. Manual of Patent Examining Procedure, U.S. Department of Commerce (1961) Sec. 806.05(f) (Appendix D). This Court stated the applicable law in Powder Co. v. Powder Works, 98 U.S. 126, 137. Here, however, the New Jersey Supreme Court has drawn a non-existing separation between product, process and use, in spite of the fact that in 1960, the United States Patent Office had found that they constituted part of a single invention.

Johnson & Johnson has enjoyed a full monopoly since 1959, with the broad product claim of U.S.P. 2,878,263. Assignment of the two later patents, which issued in 1963 and 1965 respectively, will result in unconstitutionally rewarding the employer with an extension of the monopoly for an additional six-year period.

The New Jersey Supreme Court operates on the erroneous assumption that breadth of monopoly depends on the number of claims, and states:

> "Ortho was under no obligation to broaden its claims beyond its claim to the compound itself." (Appendix B, 5a)

This holding is clearly erroneous. The crux of the matter is that 35 U.S.C. 112 permits to define a single invention with "one or more claims," which may fall into more than one of the statutory classes of product, process and use. Manual of Patent Examining Procedure, U.S. Department of Commerce, Sec. 706.03(k) (Appendix D). No relationship exists between the number of claims and the breadth of the monopoly. The reverse is generally true. A single claim, as in this case, gives the broadest possible monopoly. Additional claims are frequently included to narrow the scope of the monopoly, in the event the broadest claim, later, is found to be anticipated. Ellis, Patent Claims, Baker, Voorhis & Co. (1949) at 141, 588.

Contrary to the holding of the New Jersey Supreme Court, a product claim, as respondents obtained in 1959, is the broadest and most comprehensive. In General Electric Co. v. Wabash Appliance Corp., 304 U.S. 364, 373, 374, this Court noted that a product claim seeks to monopolize the product, no matter how created. A product claim gives the patentee a monopoly to every process which may be subsequently discovered for the manufacture of the product, and to every use of which the product is susceptible, "whether such use be known or unknown." Roberts v. Ryer, 91 U.S. 150, 157; Plummer v. Sargent, 120 U.S. 442, 448; Application of Ruschig, 343 F.2d 965, 979 (C.C.P.A. 1965). In General Electric Co. v. DeForest Radio Co., 17 F.2d 90, 98 (D.C. D. Del. 1927), the Court said:

> "There are two well established and well known modes of claiming a product of a process. One is to claim the product only as produced by the particular process. Another is to claim the product broadly, irrespective of the method of production." (Emphasis added.)

A process or use claim may be worthless in an infringement action. Ellis, loc. cit., at 450, 459. In Merrill v. Yeomans, 94 U.S. 568, this Court dismissed an infringement proceeding because the patent only claimed the process and did not include product claims. The patentee had failed to include claims on the product, which would have sustained the cause of action.

Johnson & Johnson chose the broad product claim with full awareness that it gave them the most comprehensive monopoly. In the language of their patent counsel:

> "...if you can get a claim in your patent to the product, you have an absolute monopoly on that product for a period of seventeen years, regardless of the process that might be used to prepare the compound." (Respondents' Appendix at 53a.)

Manifestly the conclusion of the New Jersey Supreme Court that substitution or addition of a process or method claim would have "<u>enlarged</u>" the monopoly, is contrary to logic, judicial decision, and to respondents' plain admissions.*

In a society where most scientists are employees of large corporations, subject to compulsory contracts, the decision of the Supreme Court of New Jersey jeopardizes our entire patent system. Unless the holding below is reversed, an employer will be encouraged to deliberately obtain patents in the name of one who is not the inventor, and after asserting

---

* The cases cited by the New Jersey Supreme Court are totally inapplicable (Appendix B, 6a et seq.). They deal with dedication to the public of subject matter described in the specification and not expressly claimed. The fundamental difference is that in this appeal, product, process and use are integral parts of a single invention. In the cited cases, on the other hand, a *non-essential* element had been described in the specification and not expressly claimed. For example, in *Brown v. Guild*, 90 U.S. 181, 185, the patentee had secured five reissue patents for each of his two earlier patents. The Court held that the non-essential element, described and not claimed, in the ten reissue patents, had been donated to the public. Similarly, *Motion Picture Patents Co. v. Universal Film Co.*, 243 U.S. 502, dealt with a patented machine and a notice restriction by the patentee that it should be used only with certain films which were not part of the invention. *Mahn v. Harwood*, 112 U.S. 354, dealt with the validity of a reissue, where the patentee sought enlargement of the monopoly, long after the issuance of the first patent, to the detriment of the public.

a monopoly for several years, will urge invalidity of its patents, at its convenience, for any technicality, including its own refusal to narrow the scope of the claims, and simultaneously will compel assignment of patents subsequently issued in the name of the real inventor. The net effect will be extension of the monopoly with benefit accruing to the employer, and a fraud on the public. This unconstitutional result is unavoidable, where no penalty is imposed, and on the other hand, the employer is rewarded with ownership of the subsequently issued patents.

(2) A Patent Must Issue in the Name of the Real Inventor.

Question 2 in this appeal involves the fundamental right of inventorship and intellectual credit guaranteed by U.S. Const., Art. I, Sec. 8, Clause 8. A patent must issue in the name of the real inventor. 35 U.S.C. 111; 37 C.F.R. 1.41 (Appendix D.)

This Court has condemned practices of fraud on the United States Patent Office. Obtaining a patent in the name of one who is not the inventor, is such gross fraud that the patent is null and void. Kennedy v. Hazelton, 128 U.S. 667. In Precision Co. v. Automotive Co., 324 U.S. 806, 816, this Court said:

> "The far reaching social and economic consequences of a patent...give the public a paramount interest in seeing that patent monopolies spring from backgrounds free from fraud or other inequitable conduct and that such monopolies are kept within their legitimate scope."

The fraud on the public, on the United States Patent Office and, of course, appellant, permeates this entire proceeding. Even assuming for the sake of argument, respondent Oroshnik conceived the idea of making the compound, as the New Jersey Supreme Court would seem to infer, he could not be the inventor. Under our laws, an invention comprises: 1) conception of idea 2) reduction to practice and 3) utility. These requirements are set forth in U.S. Const., Art. I, Sec. 8, Clause 8, 35 U.S.C. 101 and 112. In re Bremner, 182 F.2d 216 (C.C.P.A. 1950). In Manson v. Brenner, 333 F.2d 234 (C.C.P.A. 1964) cert. granted, 33 U.S.L. Week 3349, now pending before this Court, the requirement of utility of a product is not disputed. Particularly in the case of chemical inventions, the inventor is the one who reduces the idea to practice and discovers the utility of the compound. Bourne v. Jones, 114 F. Supp. 413, 418 (S.D. Fla. 1952).

Respondents admit the lack of two of the three essentials to constitute inventorship of the product, namely the process necessary to make the substance and the finding of the novel use. Thus, when Oroshnik executed the oath that he was the inventor, at the time he applied for a patent, in colorable compliance with 35 U.S.C. 115, he knowingly executed a false oath. Further, Johnson & Johnson's taking advantage of their patentee status and refusal to continue the interference proceeding because they knew they would lose in that tribunal, constitutes deliberate defiance of federal law. The discharge of the plaintiff, under the malicious accusation of "incompetency," three days after the substance proved of outstanding value as an anticonvulsant, is another instance of fraud.

The trial judge, after deciding on the matter of proprietary rights in favor of the employer, concluded, as a matter of law, that a scientist has no right of intellectual credit for his or her invention:

> "The Court: ...Such examination of the law as I have made, indicates to me that there is no right for a person, who has no property rights in an invention, to insist upon his or her name being mentioned." (R199a-22 and Original Transcript at 785.)

This monstrous and unconstitutional holding was reversed by the Appellate Division. That court held, that the right of inventorship is guaranteed both by federal law and common law principles. It properly held that credit for an invention is not alienable (Appendix C, 16a to 18a) and that an invention comprises not only conception of idea but reduction to practice and a showing of utility (Appendix C, 19a).

The Appellate Division, also, found that no conclusion may be drawn from the general jury verdict of no cause of action, because of the errors of law and the trial judge's belief that appellant was merely "annoying the respondents" and that she had no cause of action (Appendix C at 41a, 31a). The Appellate Division, found prejudicial error in the charge to the jury with respect to the entire subject matter of U.S.P. 2,878,263, not merely the one-line claim (Appendix C, 19a to 29a). It said:

> "Defendants have made no serious refutation of the proposition that if plaintiff did legally invent the compound and the process for making it, she possessed a professional right of intellectual credit... The patent issued in the name of Oroshnik as inventor, although claiming

only the compound, also published the process and the idea of treating convulsions with the compound, thereby imputing all to his inventorship...(at 16a).

"The use of the product for treatment of convulsions was plainly stated in the patent and the representation of Oroshnik as inventor fairly extended to that feature of the disclosure as well as to the compound itself and the process. Defendants clearly recognized this aspect of the issues, as they were at pains to have their expert McLean testify that adding a use description to the claim would not validate it." (Emphasis added.)

The serious errors of law in the charge to the jury led the Appellate Division to reversal. The issue of deprivation of intellectual credit for everything described in the specification, was so recognized at trial, that the respondents "were at pains" to prove that plaintiff's claim of credit was groundless and valueless (Appendix C, 27a).*

Throughout trial and in their briefs before both the Appellate Division and the Supreme Court of New Jersey, respondents have continued to deprecate the invention, while simultaneously retaining the monopoly on the public (Appendix C at 28a). Now the Supreme Court of New Jersey, in reversing the Appellate Division, in favor of Johnson & Johnson, summarily concludes that the serious errors of law in the charge

---

* Respondents produced an expert to testify that use claims could not be obtained, and that the process of making the compound was not patentable. The Appellate Division, however, reversing, found that, contrary to the respondents' position, claims on a novel use may be obtained, and that their reliance on a repealed statute and an old 1943 decision, cannot be the law today. (Appendix C, 20a).

to the jury, are "not material" (Appendix B, 6a).
This conclusion is reached in spite of the fact that
respondents recognized the issues at trial and "were
at pains" to prove that the entire invention, product,
process and use, was worthless. The incredible conclusion is reached merely because two patents have
issued, some two and three years after trial, in
appellant's name, and because appellant has not proven
special damages. In direct contrast, the Appellate
Division had found that the mere issuance of the
later patents, would not relieve respondents of liability
and that proof of special damages was not essential
(Appendix C, 32a).

The facts are essentially undisputed. Appellant
had conducted extensive research in the same field of
the invention involved in this appeal. A patent, U.S.P.
2,776,289 (Exh. P-7, R273a) in her sole name, unequivocally demonstrates her expertise in the same
field, prior to her employment with Johnson & Johnson.
The Appellate Division has so described the circumstances surrounding the invention and the relationship
with appellant's prior field of research (Appendix C,
at 11a):

> "...She began to use her spare time at
> Ortho on a problem which had long defied organic
> chemists although considerable work had been
> done on it. The making of a substance which
> would contain the beneficial qualities of bar-
> biturates but not their undesirable toxic and
> habituating characteristics. It is her contention
> that she succeeded at Ortho in doing so and
> that the patent which issued to Ortho by the
> United States Patent Office on March 17, 1959
> in the name of William Oroshnik as inventor
> (No. 2,878,263), claiming the compound, "4-
> methyl 4-phenyl 5-pyrazolone" resulted from
> her discovery of that compound."

The Appellate Division also found that appellant on January 26, 1956, at one of the company seminars, has disclosed her idea of making the product. The written exhibit corroborated her testimony (Appendix C, 12a). In April 1956, after several unsuccessful experiments, she succeeded in making the substance. Pharmacological testing established the value as an anticonvulsant. Three days later, on April 25, 1956, she was summarily discharged.

There is evidence that the legal staff of Johnson & Johnson prepared the patent application on the novel anticonvulsant at the very time of the discharge. They, however, kept it concealed, delayed and did not file the patent application in the United States Patent Office, until two years later. The reason for the delay is that at the time of the discharge, April 1956, Johnson & Johnson wished to conceal appellant's scientific contributions. The concealment went as far as denying under oath the existence of patent applications covering appellant's invention. (Affidavit of November 21, 1960; Testimony of April 12, 1961.)

The attorneys for Johnson & Johnson have admitted they knew that the plaintiff would claim to be the inventor, but concealed the filing of the patent application from her because of the litigation:

> "We did not consult her about it, because at that time, Dr. Misani had been discharged from employment and we were involved in litigation with her." (March 23, 1962 Transcript at 19.)

Although the facts surrounding the delay in filing and concealment of the invention, for malicious motives, are undisputed, the New Jersey courts have held that an employer has the absolute right to conceal employees' inventions, "<u>throw them out of the window</u>" (R66a) and "<u>scrap them at its unfettered will</u>" and later seek patent rights. Appellant submits that this holding nullifies our constitutional policy of promoting the progress of science and useful arts, U.S. Const., Art I, Sec. 8, Clause 8 and 35 U.S.C. 102(c). In <u>Woodbridge</u> v. <u>United States</u>, 263 U.S. 50, this Court so construed R.S. 4886, the predecessor of 35 U.S.C. 102(c):

> "Any practice by which the inventor deliberately and without excuse postpones beyond the date of the actual invention, the beginning of the term of the monopoly and puts off the free public enjoyment of the useful invention is an evasion of the statute."

Johnson & Johnson's patent staff has admitted having copied from appellant's research records, in her handwriting, the subject matter of U.S.P. 2,878,263, which is in the name of Oroshnik. On the crucial question of decision as to inventorship, the patent staff of Johnson & Johnson has no explanation, except that Oroshnik told them that he had "<u>conceived the idea</u>" (Appendix C, 38a). It is this oral self-serving declaration on the part of Oroshnik, with no proof whatsoever, neither from other witnesses, nor any written documents, which, according to the New Jersey Supreme Court, relieves Johnson & Johnson from liability (Appendix B, 5a).

The express refusal of the New Jersey courts to apply federal law, in a field of federal pre-emption, is manifest from the denial of appellant's motion for judgment on the issue of inventorship (Appendix C, at 33a). Appellant has urged application of rule of the United States Patent Office, 37 C.F.R. 1.216(a) (4) (Appendix D) which makes the testimony of a party, as to his conception of idea, inadmissible, unless corroborated by authentic exhibits or some witnesses. Respondent Oroshnik's testimony as to his alleged conception of idea of making the compound, was totally uncorroborated, and, of course, inadmissible. Application of federal law would have entitled appellant to her motion for judgment. U.S. Const., Art VI; Sperry v. Florida, 373 U.S. 379.

The rule is substantive, designed to prevent perjury and analogous to the two-witness requirement in the law of treason. Cramer v. United States, 325 U.S. 1. Conception of idea is an act of the mind and must be corroborated by extrinsic evidence. Otherwise each party could fabricate dates and facts to suit his convenience. Radio Corporation of America v. Philco Corporation, 201 F. Supp. 135, 149 (E.D. Pa. 1961); Townsend v. Smith, 36 F.2d 292, 295 (C.C.P.A. 1929); 2 Walker, Patents, (Secs. 201, 206, Deller's Ed. 1937).

The trial judge expressly disregarded federal law ("I am not interested in the rules." R130a to R131a), permitted Oroshnik to testify as to his alleged conception of idea and denied appellant's request of a special verdict and submitting written interrogatories to the jury. One of the denied interrogatories was:

"Who conceived the idea?" (R213a)

The Appellate Division found error in the denial. It said:

"The foregoing discussion, incidentally, points up the desirability in such a case as this of requesting a special verdict from the jury on the issue of the identity of the inventor." Plaintiff made such a request below (Appendix C, at 31a).

In spite of the finding by the Appellate Division, the Supreme Court of New Jersey draws an inference in favor of respondent Oroshnik, from the general jury verdict of no cause of action. This conclusion is not only unwarranted, but an express arrogation of the authority given to Congress by the Constitution. If this holding is not reversed, an employer will be permitted and encouraged to evade federal law, defeat an adjudication of inventorship by the United States Patent Office, and win a contest according to employer-made rules.

(3) A Patentee Who Has Not Disclaimed His Own Patent Nor Corrected the Errors, May Not Argue in Derogation of His Own Grant.

According to the New Jersey courts, an employer may refuse to disclaim a patent, 35 U.S.C. 253, refuse to limit the scope of the monopoly, 35 U.S.C. 251, continue to assert the broad monopoly upon the public, and later may argue invalidity of its own patent, to defeat the employee's cause of action (Appendix C, 15a; Appendix B, 5a). This holding effectively destroys our constitutional policy, invalidates 35 U.S.C. 251 and 253 and must be reversed.

Johnson & Johnson's defiance of federal law is manifest from their language:

> "We could [disclaim], but that is solely within our privilege to do so or not to do so, we are the owners of the patent" (R163a).

Johnson & Johnson had the duty to disclaim the patent or limit the broad scope of the product claim, as early as January 1961, when the United States Patent Office notified the parties that the interference proceeding, based on the product claim, would be dissolved. Ensten v. Simon, Ascher & Co., 282 U.S. 445, Altoona Theatres v. Tri-Ergon Corp., 294 U.S. 477, 490. Appellant has urged that a party who continues to enjoy the benefits under a patent, is not permitted to argue invalidity, to defeat the adversary's cause of action. Kinsman v. Parkhurst, 18 How. (59 U.S.) 289, 293; United States v. Harvey Steel Co., 196 U.S. 310, 316; Sola Electric Co. v. Jefferson Co., 317 U.S. 173, 175. Appellant's argument, however, has been rejected.

Contrary to the unsupported conclusion of the New Jersey Supreme Court, appellant never conceded that U.S.P. 2,878,263 is invalid as to subject matter.* The Appellate Division properly passed upon "the narrow question of the validity of the patent claim and remedying the defects" (Appendix C, 29a, 18a).

In flagrant disregard of federal law, the trial judge charged the jury that appellant had no cause of action because U.S.P. 2,878,263 was "invalid, legally invalid," and that Johnson & Johnson had no duty to correct the error:

> "They own it...that is their business, that is not her business" (R66a; R55a to R57a).

---

* Appellant repeatedly said:
 "The subject matter of the patent is perfectly good...The patent is valid, although the claim is defective." (R75a-1-24; R75a-23-5).

Also the Supreme Court of New Jersey has accepted Johnson & Johnson's assertion of invalidity, not accompanied by a disclaimer.

(4) The Refusal to Permit Appellant to Adduce Evidence as to the Constitutionality of the Contract, Violates Due Process of Law.

1. One of the issues in this appeal is the comprehensive compulsory contract, an agreement to assign inventions to the employer, enforced against appellant in this second case. The blanket refusal to permit appellant to introduce evidence in support of her contention that the contract as enforced is unconstitutional, amounts to a denial of due process of law (R125a; R237a).

In order to justify the refusal to permit evidence of unconstitutional application, the New Jersey courts summarily apply the doctrine of res judicata as if the issues had been disposed of in the first case (Appendix B, 4a). The crux of the matter, however, is that the doctrine of res judicata has been applied in vacuo, because the same contract was not even mentioned in the courts' opinions in the first case. Further, appellant has sought and respondents have opposed at every stage* consolidation of the two cases. Thus, the doctrine of res judicata rewards Johnson & Johnson for splitting the litigation and taking conflicting positions at different stages.

---

* As late as her Petition for Certiorari, Docket No. 819, Fall Term, 1962, appellant requested this Court to postpone consideration of her Petition until the second case was decided by the New Jersey courts.

The contract in issue is shown at page 8 of the Petition for Certiorari, Docket No. 819, Fall Term, 1962, in the first case. It was executed on February 28, 1955, two months after beginning of employment. The contract is of the "adhesion type," and shows the evils of a society where the employer imposes on a research scientist the contract of its liking, with prospective application ad infinitum. The contract is not limited to specific work assigned, but strips the employee of all inventions and ideas, present, past and to a great extent, even future inventions and ideas, after termination of employment. Included in the contract are Ortho Pharmaceutical, Johnson & Johnson and the family of some eighty subsidiaries, including the foreign subsidiaries.

As presently enforced by the New Jersey courts, the employer gives nothing to the employee, employment "at will," "for five minutes" (R125a; Court's opinion, attached to Petition for Certification in the first case, at 82a). The employee, however, is bound to assign to anyone of the Johnson & Johnson subsidiaries, her inventions, improvements, ideas and patents, with no limitation in time.

The two patents in issue are the result of appellant's legal training after the discharge by Johnson & Johnson. Unable to find employment in her field, appellant has completed Law School, passed Bar Examinations, and is registered to practice before the United States Patent Office. Appellant has prepared and prosecuted herself the two patent applications which issued as U.S.P. 3,079,397 and U.S.P. 3,166,475.

The consideration by the employer in the written contract was left in the ambiguous term: "In view of my employment and wages and salary paid." On February 28, 1955, appellant was induced to sign under the representation that the employment could not be terminated except for good and just cause, after notice and hearing. In the first case, however, the trial judge dismissed the contract count on the ground that the contract of employment was terminable "at will," at any time, for no reason.

He found that there was no cause for the discharge, no foundation for the charge of incompetency, that the plaintiff had not been given a hearing, but concluded that the contract was terminable at will and she had no right to a hearing. (Court's opinion in the first case at 50a, 53a, 67a, 75a.) In reaching the conclusion of employment "at will," the judge did not consider the written contract in issue here, and ignored the promises made at the time the contract was executed. Manifestly the cause of action for breach of the employment contract would have been sustained, if the promises made at the time the contract was executed, had been considered.

The crux of our patent policy is the incentive to the individual inventor. The rationalization for the granting of a monopoly rests upon the assumption that rewarding the individual inventor for limited times serves the public interest and protects and encourages initiative, talent and inventive ability. The monstrous holding of the New Jersey courts that an individual must assign all her inventions, before and after employment, to the employer, in return for nothing from the employer, expressly destroys our constitutional policy.

2. On the matter of rights of an employer to the inventions of an employee, with and without a contract of assignment of inventions, the New Jersey courts are in striking conflict with the decisions of this Court. Normally, the employee retains title of his inventions,

and the employer gets, at the most, a shopright.
A contract to assign must be supported by adequate
consideration flowing from the employer to the
employee. At no time an employee who has been
discharged for no reason, "at will," has been compelled to assign his inventions to the employer, after
termination of employment. The contract has come
to an end. Hapgood v. Hewitt, 119 U.S. 226; U.S. v.
Dubilier Condenser Corp., 289 U.S. 178; Standard Parts
Co. v. Peck, 264 U.S. 52.

3. The New Jersey courts are also in conflict with
the holdings from other jurisdictions as well as prior
holdings of the New Jersey courts. Kinkade v. N.Y.
Shipbuilding Corp., 21 N.J. 362 (1956); Texas Co. v.
Gulf Refining Co., 26 F.2d 394 (5th Cir. 1928);
Cahill v. Regan, 5 N.Y. 2nd 292, 297, 157 N.E. 2nd
505, 508 (Ct. App. N.Y. 1959); Triumph Electric Co.
v. Thullen, 228 Fed. 762 (E.D. Pa. 1916); Simmons
v. California Institute of Technology, 194 P.2d 521
(Sup. Ct. Cal. 1948); aff'd 34 Cal. 2nd 264, 209 P.2d
581 (1949).

4. The splitting of the litigation and application of
the doctrine of res judicata in the second case, have
operated as a denial of due process of law as to all
the issues involved, in this nine-year litigation. In
the first case, appellant urged fraud at the hiring,
namely that she was hired presumably to conduct
research work in Medicinal Chemistry, with no
limitation as to a specific project, but with the undis-
closed motive of exploiting her prior expertise in a
very limited field, and then discharging her. The trial
judge, however, in the first case, refused to consider
the connection in subject matter between U.S.P.
2,878,263 and appellant's specialized prior knowledge.
Similarly, the malicious accusation of "incompetency"
in the first case, became, in this second case, that

appellant of course "<u>was a scientist who could use
her head and knowledge,</u>" as good as any other senior
chemist (R62a; Appendix B, 4a). The destruction of
a scientist's professional status has never been considered by the New Jersey courts, nor submitted to
a jury.

Conclusion

Plenary review of the issues involved in this
appeal is respectfully urged. All the questions are
of profound importance in a society where the individual scientist is subject to compulsory "adhesion-
type" contracts, and where the employer may, under
the shield of state law, enlarge the scope of the
patent monopoly.

The conflict between the printed opinions of the
Appellate Division and the Supreme Court of New
Jersey, by itself, merits consideration. If appellant has chosen the improper route for seeking
review, the Court is respectfully urged to grant
certiorari.

Respectfully submitted,

FERNANDA MISANI
Plaintiff-Appellant, pro se
40 Tamaques Way
Westfield, New Jersey

APPENDIX A

JUDGMENT

This cause having been duly argued before this Court by Mrs. Fernanda Misani (Fiordalisi), counsel for appellant and Mr. Clyde A. Szuch and Mr. Stanley C. Smoyer, counsel for the respondent, and the Court having considered the same,

It is hereupon ordered and adjudged that the judgment of the said Superior Court, Appellate Division is affirmed in part and reversed in part; and it is further ordered that this mandate shall issue ten days hereafter, unless an application for rehearing shall have been granted or is pending, or unless otherwise ordered by this Court, and that the record be remitted to the Superior Court, Appellate Division to be there proceeded with in accordance with the rules and practice relating to that court, consistent with the opinion of this Court.

WITNESS the Honorable Joseph Weintraub, Chief Justice, at Trenton on the first day of June, 1965.

s/ John H. Gildea
Clerk of the Supreme Court

FILED
June 1, 1965
John H. Gildea
Clerk

A TRUE COPY
s/ John H. Gildea,
Clerk

PETITION FOR REHEARING

No Justice who voted with the majority having moved a reconsideration the petition for rehearing is denied.

Witness, the Honorable Joseph Weintraub, Chief Justice, at Trenton, this first day of July, 1965.

s/ John H. Gildea
Clerk

F I L E D
July 1, 1965
John H. Gildea
Clerk

APPENDIX B

Opinion of the Supreme Court of New Jersey

PER CURIAM. The trial court dismissed the plaintiff's action as against some of the defendants and the jury returned a general verdict in favor of the remaining defendants. On appeal, the Appellate Division ordered a new trial as to the defendants Ortho, Oroshnik and Johnson & Johnson. See 83 *N. J. Super.* 1 (1964). Thereafter, we granted cross-petitions for certification. 43 *N. J.* 264 (1964).

[1, 2] The plaintiff was employed by Ortho in January 1955 after she had responded to an advertisement seeking an organic chemist to perform "research in synthetic medicinal chemistry" of "basic character." Shortly thereafter she signed an agreement which assigned to Ortho all of her rights in inventions, improvements and ideas which she might make or conceive during her employment. The Appellate Division held that this was a valid and binding agreement and that under *its* terms Ortho owned outright any inventions made or conceived by the plaintiff while in its employ and was free to use or discard them "or to patent them or scrap them, wholly or partly, at its unfettered will." 83 *N. J. Super.*, at pp. 12–13. We agree with this holding. See *Patent & Licensing Corp. v. Olsen*, 188 *F. 2d* 522, 525 (2 *Cir.* 1951); *Paley v. Du Pont Rayon Co.*, 71 *F. 2d* 856, 858 (7 *Cir.* 1934); *Goodyear Tire & Rubber Co. v. Miller*, 22 *F. 2d* 353, 355 (9 *Cir.* 1927); see also *Universal Winding Co. v. Clarke*, 108 *F. Supp.* 329 (*D. Conn.* 1952); *Restatement (Second)*, *Agency* § 397, comment a (1958).

Appendix B—Opinion of the Supreme Court of New Jersey

[3] The plaintiff continued as an employee of Ortho until April 25, 1956 on which date her employment was terminated. In 1957 she instituted an action at law against Ortho and others claiming that her employment was terminable only for cause, economic necessity or general incapacity and asserting charges of various nature. After a trial before Judge Barger sitting without a jury, her action was dismissed. On appeal, the dismissal was sustained by the Appellate Division in an opinion which has not been published in the reports and we denied certification. 38 *N. J.* 304 (1962). Although the plaintiff has sought to reassert her claim that her employment was wrongfully terminated, the Appellate Division in the present proceeding properly held that she was barred from doing so. See 83 *N. J. Super.*, at *p.* 13. Under settled principles of *res judicata*, all of the matters which were decided adversely to her by Judge Barger are now foreclosed to her. See *Washington Tp. v. Gould*, 39 *N. J.* 527, 533 (1963); *New Jersey Highway Authority v. Renner*, 18 *N. J.* 485, 493 (1955).

[4] In 1959 Ortho obtained patent No. 2,878,263 on compound 4-methyl-4-phenyl-5-pyrazolone. This patent named William Oroshnik as inventor and assignor to Ortho. Oroshnik was the plaintiff's supervisor while she was in Ortho's employ. He testified that he had conceived the idea for the pyrazolone compound and had directed the plaintiff to make it; he acknowledged that she had worked out the details of the process but that this was what he would expect of any senior chemist functioning under his direction and possessing basic chemical know-how. See 83 *N. J. Super.*, at *p.* 11. The plaintiff testified that the idea was hers and she contends that, notwithstanding her transfer of ownership to Ortho, she was entitled to be named as inventor and may assert a tort claim grounded on the naming of Oroshnik rather than her. During the trial, the plaintiff conceded that the patent issued on the compound *per se* was invalid (83 *N. J. Super.*, at *p.* 17); she acknowledged that the patent on the compound had been anticipated by the *Beilstein* reference (83

Appendix B—Opinion of the Supreme Court of New Jersey

N. J. Super., at *p.* 16) and contended, however, that if Ortho had broadened its application so as to include claims to the process in making the compound and to the use of the compound, it could have obtained a valid patent. But Ortho was under no obligation to broaden its claims beyond its claim to the compound itself and it unequivocally asserts before us, as it did before the lower courts, that patent No. 2,878,263 on the compound itself is invalid. Although the plaintiff now seeks before us to withdraw the concession below on the basis of which the trial was conducted, and to advance the contention that the patent on the compound *per se* is not invalid, we consider that she is in no just position to do so. See *State v. Atlantic City Electric Co.*, 23 *N. J.* 259, 264 (1957); *Gebhardt v. Public Service Coord. Transport*, 48 *N. J. Super.* 173, 182 (*App. Div.* 1957), certif. denied 25 *N. J.* 540 (1958). See also *Journeymen Barbers, etc., Local 687 v. Pollino*, 22 *N. J.* 389, 395 (1956); *Beckmann v. Township of Teaneck*, 6 *N. J.* 530, 537 (1951).

In 1963 the plaintiff herself obtained patent No. 3,079,397 on the process and in 1965 she obtained patent No. 3,166,475 on the use or "method for relieving convulsions." During the trial she introduced no substantial testimony to indicate that she had suffered any special damage from the omission of her name and the inclusion of Oroshnik's name in patent No. 2,878,263. *Cf. Prosser, Torts* § 122 (3d ed. 1964); 1 *Harper & James, Torts* §§ 6.1, 6.4 (1956). And in the light of the whole record including the trial court's charge, we believe that the jury's verdict may fairly be read as evidencing its finding that there had been no lack of good faith in connection with the application for the patent and that, as between the plaintiff and Oroshnik, the latter rather than the former conceived the idea for the compound. Notwithstanding the afore-mentioned considerations pointing against her asserted claim for damages, the Appellate Division concluded that the plaintiff was entitled to a new trial. In reaching this conclusion, it expressed the view that the representation in the patent of Oroshnik as inventor is to be taken as extending to the process and use as well as to the compound itself (83 *N. J. Super.*, at *p.* 24); we are satisfied that that view was erroneous and that the ensuing grant of a new trial to the plaintiff was equally erroneous.

[5, 6] While the Appellate Division soundly found on the record before it that the plaintiff could not sustain any claim for damages insofar as inventorship credit for the compound itself was concerned (83 *N. J. Super.*, at *p.* 17), it proceeded to set aside the jury's verdict on the finding that there had been erroneous instruction concerning patentability of the process as distinct from the compound (83 *N. J. Super.*, at *pp.* 20–22) and erroneous failure to instruct concerning patentability of a novel use of the compound (83 *N. J. Super.*, at *pp.* 24–25). But those matters were not material and caused no prejudice in the case at hand unless there was actually an actionable misrepresentation that Oroshnik rather than the plaintiff was the inventor insofar as process and use were concerned. The Appellate Division in effect made such a finding when it stated that although the patent issued to Ortho in the name of Oroshnik as inventor admittedly claimed only the compound, it also published "the process and the idea of treating convulsions with the compound, thereby imputing all to his inventorship." 83 *N. J. Super.*, at *p.* 14; see also 83 *N. J. Super.*, at *p.* 24. Nothing in the record before us affirmatively supports any such imputation and the infringement cases, while not controlling here, contain much judicial language to indicate that no representation of inventorship may fairly be said to attach to matters of process and use set forth in the specification but not in the patent claim itself. See 35 *U. S. C. A.* § 112 (1954); *Brown v. Guild*, 23 *Wall.* 181, 224–225, 90 *U. S.* 181, 224–225, 23 *L. Ed.* 161, 170 (1874); *Mahn v. Harwood*, 112 *U. S.* 354, 360–361, 5 *S. Ct.* 174, 28 *L. Ed.* 665, 668 (1884); *Motion Picture Patents Co. v. Universal Film Mfg. Co.*, 243 *U. S.* 502, 510, 37 *S. Ct.* 416, 61 *L. Ed.* 871, 876 (1917); *General Electric Co. v. Wabash Appliance Corp.*, 304 *U. S.* 364, 368–369, 52 *S. Ct.* 899, 82 *L. Ed.* 1402, 1405 (1938); *Graver*

Appendix B—Opinion of the Supreme Court of New Jersey

Tank & Mfg. Co. v. Linde Air Prod. Co., 336 *U. S.* 271, 277, 69 *S. Ct.* 535, 93 *L. Ed.* 672, 677–678 (1949), aff'd on rehearing. 339 *U. S.* 605, 70 *S. Ct.* 854, 94 *L. Ed.* 1097 (1950). In any event, the asserted tort claim grounded on an alleged misrepresentation depriving inventorship credit as to process and use, appears to be a relatively novel one in the law, and while we may be prepared to recognize such a claim where the circumstances justly call for it, we are not prepared to recognize it where, as here, the reliance is placed, not on any express misrepresentation of inventorship as to process and use, but on a supposed implication thereof from a patent claim which was carefully limited to the compound itself and was conceded throughout the trial to be invalid as such.

In *Mahn v. Harwood, supra,* the Court pointed out that in taking out a patent there must be a specific claim and that matters set forth in the specification but not embraced in the specific claim "are not claimed by the patentee, at least, not claimed in and by that patent"; in the course of his opinion for the Court, Justice Bradley had this to say:

"The public is notified and informed, by the most solemn act on the part of the patentee, that his claim to invention is for such and such an element or combination and for nothing more. Of course, what is not claimed is public property. The presumption is, and such is generally the fact, that what is not claimed was not invented by the patentee, but was known and used before he made his invention. But, whether so or not, his own act has made it public property, if it was not so before. The patent itself, as soon as it is issued, is the evidence of this. The public has the undoubted right to use and it is to be presumed does use, what is not specifically claimed in the patent." 112 *U. S.,* at *p.* 361, 5 *S. Ct.,* at *p.* 178, 28 *L. Ed.,* at *p.* 668

In *Straussler v. United States,* 290 *F. 2d* 827 (*Ct. Cl.* 1961). the court referred to the distinction between the specification and the claim and stressed the great importance of the claim as describing for the world "the area of the invention beyond which no one may go without trespassing"; it pointed out that people naturally rely on the wording of claims and "are also entitled to rely on language deliberately excluded from the claims because this tends to indicate what

Appendix B—Opinion of the Supreme Court of New Jersey

the inventor has agreed his invention is not." 290 *F. 2d,* at p. 831. Patent No. 2.878,263 fairly evidences on its face that no inventive claim was made on Oroshnik's behalf beyond the compound itself. Thus the opening paragraph states that the invention "relates to 4-methyl-4-phenyl-5-pyrazolone" and that "the novel compound" possesses particular value as an anticonvulsant and is useful in the treatment of epilepsy. Still later the statement is made that the object of the invention is to provide "a new compound" which has a high protective index and is nontoxic in use over a long period of time, and that another object of the invention is to provide "a new compound" for use in the treatment of epilepsy. The concluding portion explicitly states that "What is claimed is: The compound 4-methyl-4-phenyl-5-pyrazolone."

We have considered the many contentions made by the plaintiff in her briefs and at oral argument and have concluded that none of them warrants appellate disturbance of the trial court's dismissal of her action against some of the defendants and the jury's verdict in favor of the remaining defendants. Accordingly, the Appellate Division's decision insofar as it ordered a new trial as to the defendants Ortho, Oroshnik and Johnson & Johnson is:

Reversed and the judgment entered in the trial court in favor of all of the defendants is reinstated. No costs.

For reversal — Chief Justice WEINTRAUB, and Justices JACOBS, FRANCIS, PROCTOR, HALL and HANEMAN—6.

For affirmance—None.

APPENDIX C
Opinion of Superior Court of New Jersey, Appellate Division

(Filed March 11, 1964.)

CONFORD, S.J.A.D.

Plaintiff, formerly employed by the defendant, Ortho Pharmaceutical Corp., as a research chemist, brought this action for damages by reason of Ortho's designation of a different person as "inventor" in its application for a patent which eventually was issued to it on a pharmaceutical compound, the idea, manufacturing process and novel use of which was allegedly discovered by plaintiff. The gravamen of the suit is that defendant's action thereby deprived plaintiff of professional credit for the invention. The complaint and pretrial order also assert injury to plaintiff's alleged property rights in the invention by improper and deficient preparation and prosecution of the patent application. Joined as defendants in the action were one Oroshnik, plaintiff's direct superior at Ortho, who was designated as inventor in the patent aforementioned, and certain other supervisory employees of the company, as well as Ortho's parent corporation, Johnson & Johnson, and its board chairman, Robert W. Johnson, who were charged to have participated in the alleged wrongful acts through a Dr. Kell, patent attorney for Johnson & Johnson.

Defendants denied the allegations of the complaint, asserted that Oroshnik, not plaintiff, invented the compound, and contended that plaintiff had assigned her property rights in the patent to Ortho and that her asserted right of credit was valueless in any event because the patent itself was invalid.

Appendix C—
Opinion of the Superior Court of New Jersey,
Appellate Division.

The action was tried before a judge and jury in the Law Division. Plaintiff, not a lawyer, tried her case *pro se.* At the close of the plaintiff's case there was a dismissal by the court for lack of proof as to the defendants other than Oroshnik, Ortho and Johnson & Johnson. There is no demonstration of error on this appeal in that action, and it is herewith affirmed. The jury returned a verdict of no cause of action as to the defendants who remained in the case. Plaintiff's appeal advances numerous claims of error in rulings on proffered evidence, determinations of law during the proceedings, errors and deficiencies in the charge to the jury, and prejudicial conduct of the judge in trial of the case.

Preliminarily, note should be taken of the fact that plaintiff was unsuccessful in a prior action against the same defendants, claiming, *inter alia,* wrongful discharge from her employment with Ortho. We heretofore affirmed a judgment for defendants in that case, which was tried by a Law Division judge sitting without a jury, wherein it was held that the employment contract was at will, terminable by either party with or without cause. *Misani v. Ortho Pharmaceutical Corp.* (unreported, App. Div., May 18, 1962), certif. denied 38 N. J. 304 (1962).

Plaintiff, who is holder of a doctorate in organic chemistry, was employed by Ortho in January 1955 after she responded to an Ortho advertisement seeking an organic chemist to perform "research in synthetic medicinal chemistry" of "basic character." The following month she executed an agreement with Ortho providing in part as follows :

"FERNANDA MISANI FIORDALISI

(hereinafter called 'Employee'), in consideration of his employment, and of wages and salary paid, hereby assigns, and agrees to assign to

Appendix C—
Opinion of the Superior Court of New Jersey, Appellate Division.

ORTHO PHARMACEUTICAL CORPORATION

(hereinafter called 'Company'), or its nominee, their successors or assigns, all his rights in inventions improvements and ideas which during the period of his employment, he has made or conceived or may make or conceive, either solely or jointly with others, in the course of his employment, or in the Company's time, or with the Company's material or facilities, or relating to any subject matter with which his work for the Company is or may be concerned, or relating to any business in which the Company or any of its subsidiary or affiliated companies is involved. . . ."

Plaintiff gave testimony at the trial of the following general import. Before joining Ortho she had had experience in the preparation and synthesizing of barbiturates, among other therapeutic compounds. Specifically, she had worked with 4-4 disubstituted pyrazolones (the substance of the compound in dispute) and she had a number of scientific patents and publications to her credit. About July 1955 she began to use her spare time at Ortho in research on a problem which had long defied organic chemists although considerable work had been done on it— the making of a substance which would contain the beneficial qualities of barbiturates but not their undesirable toxic and habituating characteristics. It is her contention in this case that she succeeded at Ortho in doing so, and that the patent issued to Ortho by the U. S. Patent Office on March 17, 1959 in the name of William Oroshnik as inventor (No. 2,878,263), claiming the compound, "4-methyl-4-phenyl-5-pyrazolone," resulted from her discovery of that compound and her invention of the process of making it, also disclosed in the patent but not claimed therein independently of the compound.

Plaintiff testified that Oroshnik discouraged her efforts on the barbiturate project but she persisted. She offered in evidence notebook entries indicating preliminary unsuccessful experiments. On January 26, 1956, at a company seminar at which Oroshnik was present, as indicated by one of her working notebooks introduced in evidence, plaintiff disclosed the idea and the process for making the compound to those in attendance. Plaintiff explained in her testimony that the novelty of the process lay in the use of an acid in the final step of the production of an intermediate. She had made a search of the literature and testified it showed no "well known" process for making the intermediate at all.

Oroshnik, also a skilled research chemist, told quite a different story on the stand. He testified that at the time of plaintiff's employment at Ortho he was trying to create an anti-convulsant which would be an improvement over one then on the market. He stated that this field was one of his specialties. He directed plaintiff to salvage a common intermediate from an unsuccessful uracil project and combine it with hydrazine. She did this, and arrived at the yield of the pyrazolone compound which he was after—the subject matter of the patent. Although she worked out the details of the process, this was what he would expect of any senior chemist functioning under his direction and possessing basic chemical know-how.

Oroshnik also testified that some time after the termination of plaintiff's association with Ortho some 40 or 50 compounds, including that here in question, were sent to Dr. Kell, a Johnson & Johnson patent attorney and chemist who handled patent matters for Ortho as well. Oroshnik told Kell he conceived the idea for the pyrazolone compound and had directed plaintiff to make it, but he did not tell Kell he was the inventor of the compound or process.

Kell testified that Oroshnik told him these facts and that he, Kell, then concluded that Oroshnik was the inventor and arranged for the patenting of the compound.

A patent expert, McLean, testified on behalf of defendants that the patent was invalid because the formula of the compound was anticipated by a reference in Beilstein, a German chemical encyclopedia. He also undertook to refute plaintiff's position to the effect that if the patent claim on the compound was invalid the process of manufacture was nevertheless novel and patentable independently and that the patent claim could be validated also by amending it in the form of a claim for a method of treating convulsions by use of the compound. (We discuss the legal merits of these contentions *infra*.) McLean said the process of manufacture was neither novel or patentable, citing a number of supposedly supporting German publications which defendants offered in evidence (untranslated). McLean also gave the opinion that the suggested amendment of the patent claim as one for a proposed use for treatment of convulsions would not render it valid.

At the trial plaintiff also offered evidence of Ortho's attempt to secure a Canadian patent on the process as an admission against its position in this case, notwithstanding Ortho later withdrew it. She complains of the refusal of the trial judge to charge on the point. She also claims error in the court's refusal to allow in evidence a United States patent examiner's communication to her on a later application of her own to secure a patent on the process for the pyrazolone compound.

A previous interference proceeding brought in the United States patent office by plaintiff in relation to the Ortho patent based on her alleged priority in invention as against Oroshnik was dissolved by the agency on its own motion on the ground that the compound was not patentable by reason of anticipation by the Beilstein reference and the effect of 35 U. S. C. §102, which precludes a patent where the invention has been patented or described in a printed publication in any country more than one year prior to the date of the application for patent in the United States.

I.

One of plaintiff's principal appellate contentions is that the trial judge erred in ruling, early in the case, that ownership of the invention or inventions here involved, as distinguished from any right of plaintiff to professional *credit* for them, vested in Ortho absolutely by virtue of the assignment agreement executed by plaintiff quoted above and that consequently the company was free to use or discard these discoveries or to patent them or scrap them, wholly or partly, at its unfettered will. We think the broad language of the contract, fairly construed, clearly requires this construction; compare *Vargas v. Esquire, Inc.,* 164 F. 2d 522 (7th Cir. 1947). Plaintiff contends, alternatively, that the assignment agreement is unenforceable as inequitable because the contract of hire was for no fixed term. Where, as here, an employee is engaged for purposes of research and invention, it is generally held that an assignment agreement by the employee of the tenor of that here involved will be upheld and enforced. *Patent & Licensing Corp. v. Olsen,* 188 F. 2d 522 (2d Cir. 1951); *Paley v. Dupont Rayon Co.,* 71 F. 2d 856 (7th Cir. 1934); Annot. 153 A. L. R. 983, 998 (1944). It makes no difference that the agreement of hiring is not for any fixed term. *Goodyear Tire & Rubber Co. v. Miller,* 22 F. 2d 353 (9th Cir. 1927), reversing the lower court decision relied upon by plaintiff reported in 14 F. 2d 776 (S. D. Cal. 1926). But see *Triumph Electric Co. v. Thullen,* 228 F. 762 (E. D. Pa.

Appendix C—
Opinion of the Superior Court of New Jersey,
Appellate Division.

1916), affirmed on a narrower ground in 235 F. 74 (3rd Cir. 1916).

Even apart from the express agreement of assignment, however, the invention became the property of Ortho as a matter of law as it is indubitable that "the inventor was engaged specifically to exercise [her] inventive faculties for the employer's benefit," and the specific idea and process here assertedly conceived by plaintiff was undeniably developed while at work for Ortho. *Kinkade v. N. Y. Shipbuilding Corp.*, 21 N. J. 362, 369 (1956); *International Pulverizing Corp. v. Kidwell,* 7 N. J. Super. 345 (Ch. Div. 1950); *Standard Parts Co. v. Peck,* 264 U. S. 52 (1924).

Plaintiff also argues that enforcement of the contract against her is improper because she was wrongfully discharged. But this contention is barred by the decision of the previous case against her on that point. The issue is *res judicata.*

Plaintiff's further contention that such enforcement of the contract violates the federal constitutional provision on patents is frivolous.

We consequently hold the view that the trial court was right in ruling that insofar as plaintiff's claim was postulated on the theory that she owned the inventions of the compound or process or the idea of patenting the use of the compound as an anti-convulsant it was groundless. She legally parted with that title anticipatorily when she took the job as a research chemist employed to make such discoveries and when she executed the assignment. Ortho owed her no duty to patent, or refrain from patenting these inventions or any aspect of them, or, if it did apply for patents, to do so properly or adequately, or to repair any deficiency in the patent issued, by amendment or otherwise.

Appendix C—
Opinion of the Superior Court of New Jersey,
Appellate Division.

II.

Defendants have made no serious refutation of the proposition that if plaintiff did legally invent the compound and
the process for making it she possessed a professional right
of intellectual credit therefor even though she assigned
"all [her] rights" in inventions, ideas, etc. to Ortho, and
that a wrongful deprivation of that credit by publishing the
formula and process in a patent as the invention of another
would constitute an actionable tort. In the present case,
the patent issued to Ortho in the name of Oroshnik as
inventor, although claiming only the compound, also published the process and the idea of treating convulsions with
the compound, thereby imputing all to his inventorship.
But the trial court, although purporting to submit the issue
of credit to the jury, expressed an opinion out of the presence of the jury that there was no such right, and we think
it advisable that we lay the question to rest.

We are of the view that such an action lies, at least as
respects patentable inventions or discoveries, and that
plaintiff did not in any way surrender her rights in that
regard.

It is of the essence of the patent law and public policy
that a patent must be applied for in the name only of the
true inventor, whether issued to him or to his assignee.
35 U. S. C. §102 (f); 69 C. J. S. Patents, §84, pp. 377, 378;
Kennedy v. *Hazelton*, 128 U. S. 667, 672 (1888). The recog-
nition of such a cause of action as is presently here under
discussion obviously subserves the stated policy and tends
to prevent an imposition upon the public.

Moreover, vindication of the claim to credit on the part
of the aggrieved true inventor is readily assimilable to the
principle of an action for interference with prospective
economic advantage now thoroughly established in our
law. *Mayflower Industries* v. *Thor Corp.*, 15 N. J. Super.

Appendix C—
Opinion of the Superior Court of New Jersey, Appellate Division.

337 (Ch. Div. 1951), affirmed o.b. 9 N. J. 605 (1952). As succinctly summarized recently by the Chief Justice, "The law protects also a man's interest in reasonable expectations of economic advantage." *Harris* v. *Perl,*   N. J. (decided February 3, 1964).

Notwithstanding the fact that the area of direct economic exploitation of the invention itself has by the relationship of the parties and their agreement been appropriated exclusively unto Ortho, nevertheless plaintiff, if the true inventor, retained the valuable right of accretion to her reputation as a research scientist in organic chemistry of credit for the invention if any patent should be issued and published in connection therewith. All contemplated advantages to the company from the plaintiff's assignment of inventions and ideas were fully and reasonably utilizable by it without the need to misrepresent the inventor on a patent application. It would be unreasonable and against public policy to construe the contractual assignment as a consent by plaintiff to an abrogation of her right of credit by means of the false attribution of inventorship in the published patent to another who was not the true inventor. Compare *Vargas* v. *Esquire, Inc., supra* (164 F. 2d 522), where an artist specifically assigned all rights to his pictures and to use of his name as artist.

General understanding of the foregoing assumptions by the business and scientific community is apparent.*

---

* "* * * a United States patent is issued in the inventor's name, and although he assigns the rights to his company, his name will forever be attached to that patent. This is his indisputable claim to being an accomplished inventor, and *no one—no company*—can take this away from him. The more patents that bear his name, regardless of what he did with the rights to them, the greater is his standing in the technological community. Issued patents are tangible evidence of his worth as an inventor, and they are perfectly salable in his quest for a job wherever he goes." (emphasis by author). Barnes, "The Patent System From An Inventor's Point of View." 5 *Pat., T.M., and Copyright J.* 64, 68 (1961).

Appendix C—
Opinion of the Superior Court of New Jersey, Appellate Division.

The rationale of plaintiff's cause of action may also be supported by the analogy of an action for slander of title, in that both rest upon publication by defendant of an untrue statement which has the effect of disputing plaintiff's rightful claim to ownership of something. See *Frega v. Northern New Jersey Mtg. Assn.,* 51 N. J. Super. 331, 337-338 (App. Div. 1958). The difference, however, is that in slander of title the protected interest is the vendibility of the subject matter of the title whereas credit for a patentable invention is not alienable.

III.

As indicated, defendants contended at the trial that assuming plaintiff had a right to *credit* as inventor of the compound, as distinguished from proprietorship of the invention itself, and assuming further that she rather than Oroshnik was the inventor, she sustained no damage (or less damage than otherwise) from any deprivation of that credit by defendants' actions since the patent was invalid because anticipated by the published Beilstein reference. Indeed, their argument predicated on this point was that there was no *substantial* claim to credit even involved in the case. We find that the statute cited above, 35 U. S. C. §102 (b), concludes the issue in respect of the narrow question of the validity of the patent claim to the compound itself. It provides that a patent is not issuable if "the invention was patented or described in a printed publication in this or a foreign country * * * more than one year prior to the date of the application for patent in the United States." The Beilstein reference was in fact published more than one year prior to Ortho's application for this patent. Plaintiff conceded at the trial that the patent on the compound *per se* was invalid.

Appendix C—
Opinion of the Superior Court of New Jersey,
Appellate Division.

To the limited extent indicated, therefore, defendants' position is correct, and their point with respect to damages and the substance of a claim, insofar as the value of the inventorship *credit* depends upon the validity of the patent claim to the compound itself, was well taken.

IV.

But plaintiff argues that inventorship of the basic idea, including the process and the use of the product as an anticonvulsant, was not determinable against her under the thesis that the claim for the compound *per se* was not patentable and that the patent as issued was invalid to that limited extent. She soundly argues that inventorship comprehends not alone the conception of a novel idea but reducing it to practice. *Application of Schlittler*, 234 F. 2d 882 (C. C. P. A. 1956). The Beilstein reference was merely to what plaintiff describes as a "type" formula. It did not reveal the properties, uses or the process for making the substance. As will be seen, *infra*, claims for a process of manufacture or for a new use of a known compound are patentable independently of the compound itself.

Although patentability of the basic invention in either of the respects last noted was stressed by plaintiff below and here primarily in terms of the effect of the trial court's rulings on the question of inventorship as between herself and Oroshnik and of defendant's asserted duty to perfect its patent, we find greater pertinence thereof in terms of the effect of such rulings on the jury's resolution of the issue of whether plaintiff had a cause of action at all independently of her contest *vis a vis* Oroshnik and of whether her claim was one of any value. For reasons to be stated, we find error in the trial court's handling of these issues, and that this requires a reversal and retrial, notwithstand-

Appendix C—
Opinion of the Superior Court of New Jersey,
Appellate Division.

ing some degree of imperfection in plaintiff's communication of her position on the points to the court. We so determine partly because the issues mentioned were recognized by the court and the parties and can be said to have been tried, and partly because the interests of a just resolution of this controversy so require.

The patent statute provides that an application for a patent must contain a specification incorporating "a written description of the invention, and of the manner and process of making and using it, * * *. The specification shall conclude with one or more claims particularly pointing out and distinctly claiming the subject matter which the applicant regards as his invention." 35 U. S. C. §§111, 112. The patent protection is confined to the claim or claims stated which may be limited to the compound or apparatus, or to the process, or may claim both. *Continental Paper Bag Co.* v. *Eastern Paper Bag Co.*, 210 U. S. 405, 418-419 (1908); *Hall* v. *Keller*, 180 F. 2d 753 (5th Cir. 1950), cert. denied 340 U. S. 818 (1950). Notwithstanding the application describes both the compound and the process, the patent coverage is confined to what is expressly claimed as the invention.

By virtue of an amendment of the patent statute in 1952 patentable processes now include "a new use of a known process, machine, manufacture, composition of matter or material." 35 U. S. C. §100 (b). *Rohm & Haas Company* v. *Roberts Chemicals*, 245 F. 2d 693 (4th Cir. 1957). Previously, as noted by the court in *Rohm & Haas Company*, it was the "settled rule that a new use of an old product was not patentable." (245 F. 2d, at p. 698.) The former rule is illustrated by *In re Thuau*, 135 F. 2d 344 (C. C. P. A. 1943). That decision, relied upon by defendants here, is obviously no longer the law in view of the amendment of the statute and the illustration of its effect in *Rohm & Haas*

Company, supra. Matter of the Application of Walter L. Hack, 245 F. 2d 246 (C. C. P. A. 1957), cited by defendants as sustaining the old rule, cannot properly be understood as doing so in view of the acknowledgment therein of the unambiguous language of the statute as it now stands. The *Hack* case holds no more than that a patent sought in respect of a new use for an old product must be claimed in the form of a process claim, not a composition claim.[*]

The Ortho patent in the present case, as already seen, claimed only the compound. The patent, although not the claim, included a description of the process as well as a detailed statement of the scientific basis for the conclusion expressed therein that the "novel compound" claimed "possesses particular value as an anti-convulsant and is useful in the treatment of epilepsy." It is clear, therefore, as a matter of law, that plaintiff was *prima facie* right when she repeatedly contended below, as she does here, that the invalidation of the claim for the compound *per se* by the Beilstein reference would not have affected a claim either on the process of making the compound or the "process" of the new use of the presumably known compound as an anti-convulsant, had either or both of such claims been incorporated in the original patent or added

---

[*] To illustrate the effect of the 1952 amendment, the court in *Rohm & Haas Company, supra,* sustained the validity of a 1953 reissue patent claim reading: "The process of controlling fungus growth on living plants which comprises applying to the plants a fungicidal composition having as an active ingredient a salt of an alkylene bisdithiocarbamic acid." The original patent, issued in 1943, was drafted as a claim identical with so much of the 1953 reissue claim as reads beginning with the words "a fungicidal composition," etc. The court indicated that there was some uncertainty as to the validity of the original patent as the composition was previously known, although not used for any practical purpose until the patentee conceived of its use as a fungicide. But the 1952 statutory amendment clearly validated the 1953 reissue patent as a claim for a new use even though of a known composition.

Appendix C—
Opinion of the Superior Court of New Jersey, Appellate Division.

thereto by reissue. This assumes, of course, existence of the basic patent requirements of inventive novelty, utility and reduction to practice in such claims, and, so far as anything to the contrary may be deemed argued below or on this appeal by defendants, a jury issue as to satisfaction of such requirements was presented by the proofs.

The trial court early in the proceedings below, after ruling against plaintiff on her claim for property rights in the invention, expressly retained for trial the issue of improper representation by the patent of the *process* as the invention of Oroshnik rather than plaintiff, and stated in that regard that its patentability as "new, whether it was an invention" was relevant to the question of damages. Defendants sought to meet the issue by testimony of a patent law expert to the effect that any chemist conversant with the prior literature on the subject could have made the compound by the process plaintiff used and that it was therefore neither novel nor a patentable invention. Plaintiff testified that no one had made the specific compound—the "gem pyrazolone"—as distinguished from other pyrazolones, and that her use of an acid in the final stage of an intermediate was novel. This was not specifically controverted by defendants.

In relation to the patentability of the process plaintiff requested the court to charge the jury that: "A process is novel and patentable even if it is a combination of old elements, as long as the result is new and useful." So far as it went, this was a correct statement of the applicable law on the particular proposition thus enunciated, see *Respro* v. *Vulcan Proofing Co.*, 1 F. Supp. 45, 51-52 (E. D. N. Y. 1932); *Copease Mfg. Co.* v. *American Photocopy Equipment Co.*, 298 F. 2d 772, 781 (7th Cir. 1961). It was peculiarly relevant to the particular issue raised by defendants, and the general subject matter should therefore have been incorporated in the charge when the court was dealing with the dispute as to patentability of the process. This is so even though, in the light of the testimony adduced by defendants, the requested charge would have had to be qualified to the extent that the combination should not be obvious to one having ordinary skill in the art, *Standard Brands* v. *National Grain Yeast Corp.*, 308 U. S. 34, 38 (1939). Nothing on this particular aspect of the law is to be found in the charge at all. See *State* v. *Abbott*, 36 N. J. 63, 68 (1961).

What the court did say to the jury anent the process was the following:

> "She makes some additional claims. She says that even if she did not invent the product or even if it was not patentable, which, of course, it was not, she invented the process, the means by which it was made. Her complaint is that the company got a patent on her product, that's what she is here for, complaining about, the company did not and Dr. Oroshnik did not and Dr. Kell did not and Johnson & Johnson did not get any patent upon the process, upon the means by which this thing was made. They didn't apply for a patent. She says they should have. She says they should have done so.
>
> She has no right to tell them that they must do it. They own it, whether she invented it or whether she didn't invent it, they own it. She did it on their time with their material and they can throw it out the window if they like, as far as she is concerned. * * *
>
> The only thing she is interested in is her name on the thing, if she has a right to that.
>
> Mr. McLean testified as an expert that the process is not an invention. It is not new and there is nothing patentable in it. It is a part of the general

knowledge of chemistry available to everybody who studies the art. For this purpose he produced excerpts from chemical journals and other publications to show that all of the procedures described by Dr. Misani had been known before she used them.

Now, frankly, I don't see how you or I, as a practical matter, can decide on our own judgment whether he is right or whether he is wrong. I don't understand these publications, and some of them are in German, which makes it twice as hard. You tell me none of you read German. So I don't know what you are going to do with it. I suppose it comes down to this: You either have to believe Mr. McLean or you have to believe Dr. Misani. That is about what it comes down to, as far as that goes.

Of course, Dr. Misani, if she thought that Mr. McLean was wrong, could have produced an expert to contradict him. She did not do so, for whatever reason I do not know.

As far as that process is concerned, frankly, I don't see anything in it at all and I can't really see what claim she has.'' (emphasis added).

In the light of the pertinence of the issue of patentability of the process, as seen above, there are several prejudicially erroneous aspects of the foregoing comments. While the court was abstractly correct in telling the jury that plaintiff had no right to have the defendants patent the process insofar as any right of property on her part in the process was concerned, that subject was extraneous to the issues remaining on trial by the time of the charge as the court had earlier ruled out any property rights of the plaintiff in any aspect of the invention. A simple state-

Appendix C—
Opinion of the Superior Court of New Jersey,
Appellate Division.

ment to the jury that the court had so ruled would have sufficed. But since patentability of the process remained in the case in relation to the issue of damages (and, as defendants claimed in their summations, in relation to the gravamen of any claim for deprivation of credit at all; see *infra*), it was incumbent on the court to instruct the jury on the law relative to patentability of a process so that they might apply it to the disputed proofs and arrive at a properly considered conclusion. See, *e.g., Keyes* v. *Grant*, 118 U. S. 25, 36 (1886); *cf. Philp* v. *Nock*, 84 U. S. 460, 462 (1873). Resolution of the issue was not a simple matter of whether to "believe" defendants' expert or the plaintiff. And the absence of guidance of the jury in this regard was compounded by the court's informing them that it saw nothing in the claim in relation to the process.

Moreover, the animadversion concerning plaintiff's failure to call an "expert" to refute McLean was, in our judgment, not fully warranted. While plaintiff's position as a party naturally affected her credibility (as, of course, did also Oroshnik's), yet the comment could have been prejudicial to plaintiff. The issue of patentability of the process involved mixed questions of fact and law. On the facts, including novelty, prior art and the basic chemistry involved, plaintiff, as an advanced expert in chemistry, was presumably at least as competent as McLean. On the law, the ultimate guide to the jury was or should have been the court, even assuming propriety of testimony by the patent-lawyer witness. See III *Walker, Patents* (1937) §747, p. 2052.

The availability of patent-law experts in cases directly or collaterally involving determinations of patentability does not minimize the function of the court in instructing a jury as to the law. The question of patentability is ulti-

Appendix C—
Opinion of the Superior Court of New Jersey,
Appellate Division.

mately one of law. *Great A. & P. Tea Co.* v. *Supermarket Equip. Corp.*, 340 U. S. 147, 155 (1950) (Douglas, J., concurring); *Bergman* v. *Aluminum Lock Shingle Corp. of America*, 251 F. 2d 801, 803 (9th Cir. 1957); *Armour & Co.* v. *Wilson & Co.*, 274 F. 2d 143, 151-157 (7th Cir. 1960). This is because patentability is a "constitutional standard," *Great A. & P.*, *ubi cit.*, *supra*, reduced to a problem of statutory construction as a result of the listing of the elements of that standard in 35 U. S. C. §§102, 103. *Armour & Co.* v. *Wilson & Co.*, *supra* (274 F. 2d, at p. 156). Involved in the determination of patentability, however, is also, generally, the resolution of questions of fact, such as the state of the prior art, the nature of the inventor's discovery, and whether that discovery is novel or anticipated by the prior art. *Armour & Co.*, *ubi cit.*, *supra*; *Cee-Bee Chem. Co.* v. *Delco Chemicals*, 263 F. 2d 150, 153 (9th Cir. 1958); *Bergman* v. *Aluminum Lock Shingle Corp. of America*, *supra* 251 F. 2d, at pp. 809-810 (Pope, J., concurring). Those are peculiarly the appropriate pleas of testimony by patent experts. See *Winans* v. *The N. Y. & Erie R. Co.*, 21 How. (62 U. S.) 88, 100-101 (1859).

Helpful instructions to a jury in a case such as this, in relation to patentability of the process, would, therefore, be such as specifically required the jury to determine what had been accomplished and taught by the prior art, what if anything it was that plaintiff discovered with regard to the process, and the relationship of her discovery to such prior art. Ideally, the evidence in the case should have been brought by the court into focus as it reflected on the determination of those issues.*

---

* Obviously, technical publications in a foreign language are useless to a jury. They should be submitted in English translation, if introduced as exhibits.

Appendix C—
Opinion of the Superior Court of New Jersey, Appellate Division.

Our reversal in this case in relation to the matter of patentability of the process is not based, however, on the absence of an ideal charge on the law in this admittedly technical and complex area, but on the failure of the instructions to make such minimal exposition of the applicable law relevant to the issue, including the general subject matter of plaintiff's request, as would enable the jury properly to discharge its function other than by sheer reaction to the personalities of plaintiff and the opposing expert.

We next consider the failure of the trial court to charge the jury the law respecting patentability of the invention in respect of a novel use claim, particularly in the light of its frequent comments during the trial that amending the patent claim for that purpose was no concern of plaintiff. Agreed that insofar as plaintiff was claiming a duty to her by defendants to perfect the original patent claim, she was wrong. But insofar as the claim to deprivation of *credit* was concerned, patentability of a novel use claim had the same materiality to the issues as patentability of the process and of the compound. The use of the product for treatment of convulsions was plainly stated in the patent, and the representation of Oroshnik as inventor fairly extended to that feature of the disclosure as well as to the compound itself and the process. Defendants clearly recognized this aspect of the issues, as they were at pains to have their expert McLean testify that adding a use description to the claim would not validate it. McLean, however, relied on *In re Thuau, supra,* but we have seen that the effect of that decision was overcome by the 1952 amendment of the statute permitting process claims in the form of new uses of known compositions if framed as such. To the extent that defendants consistently contended that plaintiff's claim to credit was groundless and valueless

Appendix C—
Opinion of the Superior Court of New Jersey,
Appellate Division.

because there was no patent validity in her invention,* she had the right to attempt to show the contrary by proving that what was disclosed in the patent and attributed to the inventorship of Oroshnik contained patentable subject matter.

All that the trial court said to the jury in relation to the issue of patentability of the invention as a process or method claim for the new use of the compound as an anti-convulsant was this:

"I have already mentioned the fact that Dr. Misani has repeatedly pressed the idea that Ortho could get a good patent if they changed the wording of the claim; and we have had evidence that they couldn't. Well, frankly, it doesn't make any difference whether they could or whether they couldn't. That is not what the suit is about. As I told you before, that's none of her business."

Not only did this constitute a failure to instruct the jury on the applicable law, but it took the issue of patentability of the alleged new use out of the case completely. And this notwithstanding defendants had recognized its materiality in relation to the value and gravamen of plain-

---

* *E.g.*, after arguing that both the compound and process were known before plaintiff's work, one of defense counsel stated in summation: "What are we talking about in the first place. It just seems too clear * * * that there was nothing of credit or value which could have been taken from the plaintiff in this situation." The other counsel said: "You cannot be deprived of credit for something which has no value. Mr. McLean * * * says that Beilstein anticipated this compound * * *. Mr. McLean also said that the addition of the word 'anti-convulsant' adds nothing to it, you couldn't get a patent by using the word 'anti-convulsant.'" (rather an oversimplification of the nature of a process claim for a new use; see *Rohm & Haas Company* v. *Roberts Chemicals, supra*).

tiff's claim of deprivation of professional credit, as distinguished from a property right in the invention, and had offered testimony on the issue pointed to that aspect of the claim. This was error, and we regard it as clearly prejudicial to plaintiff.

One of plaintiff's requests to charge included a reference to remedying defects in the patent by additional claims for matter disclosed in the patent. In her exceptions to the charge she made substantially the same objection to the omissions in the charge in respect of this point as we have voiced. Although the request to charge was incomplete and formally defective and as such was properly refused by the court, it nevertheless was sufficient, in the background of the controversy as a whole and the importance of the specific point to a just resolution of the lawsuit, to have served to alert the court to the necessity of charging the jury on the law concerning patentability of claims for new uses of known compositions. Considering also the exceptions, it was error to fail to do so. See *State* v. *Abbott, supra* (36 N. J., at p. 68); *Grammas* v. *Colasurdo,* 48 N. J. Super. 543 (App. Div. 1958); *Cf. Kreis* v. *Owens,* 38 N. J. Super. 148 (App. Div. 1955).

Defendants urge that any deficiencies in the charge in either of the respects here found faulty are immaterial in that the verdict of the jury reflects they found Oroshnik rather than plaintiff to have been the inventor. This argument is premised on part of the court's charge as to damages. The court said, in part:

"If, on the other hand, you should decide in favor of the plaintiff against any of the defendants, then you will have to decide how much.

She claims two kinds of damages. She claims compensatory damages. She says, my reputation, my good name suffered because I didn't have the credit

Appendix C—
Opinion of the Superior Court of New Jersey,
Appellate Division.

for this that I did. She brings no proof of any
special burden to her, any special loss of money.
But in this type of case if indeed you were to find
that she had suffered a diminution of her scientific
reputation* through the wrongful acts of any of
these defendants, you may allow her such reasonable
sum as will compensate her for that loss of reputation.

Of course, you don't have much to go on in the
case; there isn't much testimony. You just have to
take the general picture and see what you come up
with. If you can't find anything else, you *could*
bring in nominal damages, just if you think she was
right but she didn't get hurt. Why, *you could, I
suppose,* bring in a dollar or something like that.
Of course, you don't get to that question unless you
find in her favor." (emphasis added).

The rule is that ordinarily a verdict of no cause of
action may connote either no liability or no damages.
Kovacs v. Everett, 37 N. J. Super. 133 (App. Div. 1955),
certif. denied, 20 N. J. 466 (1956); *Carianni v. Schwenker,*
38 N. J. Super. 350, 356 (App. Div. 1955). A conclusion
that the verdict here necessarily meant a finding of no
inventorship by plaintiff *vis a vis* Oroshnik is not compelled
by the trial court's instructions. These did not purport to
make mandatory a return of nominal damages in the event
of a determination of inventorship in plaintiff but no sub-

---

* It may be noted that the more appropriate emphasis as to
plaintiff's claim of damage is that she was deprived of the accretion
to her reputation as a chemical inventor which she would presumably have gained by the publication of a patent disclosing her
inventions, here asserted to include compound, process, and new
use.

Appendix C—
Opinion of the Superior Court of New Jersey, Appellate Division.

st…ntial damages. Nominal damages was by clear inference left optional with the jury.*

But of even more importance, defendants emphasized throughout the case and particularly in summation, as already indicated that since plaintiff was not a first inventor of anything (even if she had priority as against Oroshnik) and thus had no patentable invention, her claim to credit lacked any real substance as well as value. Failure on the part of the jury because of absence of pertinent instructions in the charge to understand that the inventions disclosed in the patent could be patentable, and thus presumably valuable, with consequential value in the professional credit of inventorship therefore could readily have been a contributory factor in the determination of the jury to reject the claim of credit completely whatever they might have thought of the matter of priority as between plaintiff and Oroshnik *inter sese.* Supporting the likelihood of this is the emphasis in the charge of the invalidity of the patent as issued because of the Beilstein reference and the pervasive undertone in the charge as a whole of lack of merit in plaintiff's entire claim.**

Defendants have also argued that plaintiff cannot be deemed to have been damaged by any misrepresentation of her inventorship in the Ortho patent because she has since the trial of this action obtained a patent on the process. In the first place, the record before us does not include that fact. But even plaintiff's concession (indeed she dis-

---

* The foregoing discussion, incidentally, points up the desirability in such a case as this of requesting a special verdict from the jury on the issue of the identity of the inventor (plaintiff made such a request below).

** In respect of which we do not mean to disparage the general right of a court to comment on the testimony. But see *Ridgewood v. Sreel Investment Corp.,* 28 N. J. 121, 128, 129 (1958).

Appendix C—
Opinion of the Superior Court of New Jersey,
Appellate Division.

closed this fact in her brief) that she now has the process patent will not eliminate the issue of deprivation of credit at the retrial. This is so for several reasons.

During at least the period between the issuance of the Ortho patent and that to plaintiff there was, if plaintiff was truly the inventor, a continuing tort of misrepresentation as to her inventorship. We cannot say that the presumptive damage then done her was necessarily erased automatically by the later patent to plaintiff. Further, the coexistence of both patents casts a substantial cloud on plaintiff's reputation as the true inventor. Ortho could have eliminated this by disclaiming its patent, 35 U. S. C. §252, or amending to show plaintiff as inventor, but it has chosen not to do either. Finally, since Ortho owns the process invention under the assignment from plaintiff, it can at any time and presumably will eventually exercise its rights and compel assignment of the process invention to itself. At that point there will be no impediment to its disclaimer thereof and consequent elimination of the asserted preservation of plaintiff's reputation as the inventor.

Defendants thus have not shown that the present existence of a patent in plaintiff's name negates damage to her.

We might at this point with an eye to the impending retrial state our concurrence in the trial court's instruction to the jury that they could allow plaintiff compensatory damages even though she could demonstrate no specific special damages. The problem is somewhat comparable to that of allowability of substantial (not punitive) damages in an action for libel *per se.* Moreover, the approach of the courts is liberal in relation to a wronged plaintiff where the very nature of the subject matter makes proof of specific damages difficult. Here, the loss from impaired

Appendix C—
Opinion of the Superior Court of New Jersey, Appellate Division.

reputation for inventorship is highly correlative with the value of the patent. In the case of patented pharmaceutical products it ordinarily takes a long time to test and evaluate them and get government approval for their marketing. This should not preclude an award of reasonable damages for wrongful deprivation of credit in the interim. Compare the allowability of substantial damages on behalf of parents in an action for the wrongful death of a young child. *McStay* v. *Przychocki,* 7 N. J. 456 (1951). Cf. *Harris* v. *Perl, supra.*

Although the judgment is to be reversed for the reasons given above, some of the other grounds of appeal argued by plaintiff present questions which may arise again at the retrial and we will deal with them here to the extent deemed advisable.

V.

Plaintiff has contended that the question of the invalidity of the patent as issued was not properly triable for a number of reasons. First, it is argued that the issue was not comprehended by the pretrial order. However, we agree with defendants' ample showing that the issue was actually tried with plaintiff's acquiescence and without timely objection. R. R. 4:15-2. Miscellaneous other grounds for the argument have been examined and found without merit. An examination of the whole area of patentability of the invention in any aspect is fundamental to a just resolution of this controversy, as we have already seen, especially, as defendants argue, to the issue of damages, which was specified in the pretrial order. And insofar as plaintiff raises a number of procedural questions peculiar to federal patent practice and procedure in relation to patentability, we find them not applicable or controlling in this collateral state-court inquiry. From the adjective standpoint, we are bound only by our own rules of practice and procedure. We do recognize that we are bound by federal substantive law as to patentability, and have so indicated above.

It seems desirable that in view of the outcome of this appeal and the contents of this opinion the case should be pretried anew before the retrial.

VI.

One set of plaintiff's objections to trial rulings appertains to the law of inventorship in respect of joint work of supervisory and subordinate employees, as here.

First, plaintiff contends that the testimony of Oroshnik on the issue of discovery should have been excluded because unsupported by corroborating evidence, citing *Radio Corporation of America v. Philco Corporation*, 201 F. Supp. 135, 149 (E. D. Pa. 1961); *Harper v. Zimmerman*, 41 F. 2d 261, 265 (D. Del. 1930). However, as defendants point out, those cases involved priority of conception and are inapplicable where, as here, each of two parties alleges that he conceived the basic idea and claims to have disclosed it to the other. In the circumstances, it would have placed an impossible burden upon Oroshnik to have required him to produce a corroborating witness on the question of his conception. That witness would have had to be the plaintiff for it was to her that he alleges he disclosed the discovery. "The question of invention as between . . . [the parties] is really one of veracity. . . . The evidence of one witness may be sufficient." *C. F. Mueller Co. v. Zeregas Sons*, 12 F. 2d 517, 518 (2nd Cir. 1926); *Concrete Mixing & Conveying Co. v. R. C. Storrie & Co.*, 27 F. 2d 838, 840 (9th Cir. 1928), aff'd 282 U. S. 175 (1930). Once it is accepted, as was the tenor of defendants' proofs, that plaintiff was under the direction of Oroshnik in making the compound, then, as Kell testified, the entries of experiments in plaintiff's notebooks are corroborative of Oroshnik's claim to discovery.

Plaintiff also contends, in relation to her motion for judgment in respect of the process, that it should have been granted even if there were an open issue as to whether Oroshnik conceived the idea of the compound, since he admitted that he did not tell plaintiff what process to use in developing the compound. This argument, and the citation of *Pembroke v. Sulger*, 265 F. 996, 998 (Ct. App. D. C. 1920) and *Forgie v. Oil Well Supply Co.*, 58 F. 871, 876 (3rd Cir. 1893) in support thereof, are met by the circumstance that the cited cases dealt with situations where only the result to be accomplished was disclosed to the subordinate. Here, Oroshnik testified:

> "I assigned to Dr. Misani, therefore, I gave Dr. Misani a specific directive, since we were dropping the urecil project, to utilize whatever of the intermediate that she had accumulated, to condense that with hydrazine to give us the pyrazolones which would theoretically add to our anticonvulsant program."

This was more than simply telling plaintiff what result Oroshnik wanted. But the real issue here implicated is whether there was a jury question as to the existence of any element of novelty over the prior art in plaintiff's working out of the process. We hold defendants' proofs clearly did create such an issue for the jury.

Plaintiff makes a general attack on the portion of the charge dealing with the question of inventorship as arising between a superior and subordinate in an employment

Appendix C—
Opinion of the Superior Court of New Jersey,
Appellate Division.

relationship. The court's charge on this point consisted to a large extent of a quotation from 69 C. J. S., Patents §92 (a), (b), which we find basically supported by the authorities cited therein and need not discuss here. The charge adequately conveyed to the jury the concept that the supervisor can get help from a skilled subordinate in reducing his conception to practice and still be considered the inventor. The charge as given, moreover, was actually more favorable to plaintiff than it need have been. Basically, this was to the effect that where the idea of an invention is disclosed to an employee by the employer (or to a subordinate by a supervisor), there is a presumption that the final product arising from this collaboration is the invention of the employer. 69 C. J. S., Patents §92 (b), pp. 421-22. But in so instructing the jury the court was restricting the applicability of this presumption to the issue as to the good faith of Kell in deciding that Oroshnik was the inventor. Actually, the defendants were entitled to the benefit of the presumption on the factual question of who in reality (not merely in the mind of Kell) was the inventor. See *Riehm* v. *Hambleton*, 53 F. Supp. 328 (D. Mass. 1943).

Citing *Herrmann* v. *Otken*, 201 F. 2d 909 (C. C. P. A. 1953), plaintiff argues that there should have been no presumption in favor of Oroshnik in this case because her academic standing was equal to that of Oroshnik. But that decision merely explains that the background and experience of the contending claimants are factors to be taken into consideration in determining which party would be more likely to have conceived the invention. That proposition does not disparage the presumption that arises after it is shown (and believed) that the employer conceived the idea and instructed the employee in its development. Note here also that the trial court specifically charged that

Appendix C—
Opinion of the Superior Court of New Jersey,
Appellate Division.

there was no presumption if the jury did not believe that Oroshnik conceived the idea.

Plaintiff also argues that there was error in admitting Kell's testimony as to the statements made to him by Oroshnik on the ground that this testimony was hearsay. However, the testimony was not hearsay in the light of the limited use for which the trial court admitted it. The statements were not admitted to prove the truth of the matter asserted in them, *i.e.*, that Oroshnik conceived the idea, but solely in relation to the issue of Kell's good faith in arriving at the conclusion that Oroshnik was the inventor and in perfecting the patent applications. The truth of the statements was irrelevant for that purpose, the only question being whether or not they were made and whether or not Kell relied on them, as affecting the liability of Johnson & Johnson, his employer.

A similar analysis validates the court's instruction with respect to Kell's testimony that he would expect a research chemist to record conception of a novel idea in her notebook. That is what Kell said he expected, and it was one of the factors upon which he based his conclusion that Oroshnik was the inventor. The judge had excluded Kell's statement that the Ortho chemists were under instructions to make such entries, and his charge was consonant with that ruling. The fact of Kell's expectation of an entry was not admitted to show the existence of such instructions to chemists or that Oroshnik was in actuality the inventor. It went only to the reasonableness of the basis for Kell's conclusion on inventorship.

Appendix C—

Opinion of the Superior Court of New Jersey, Appellate Division.

VII.

Several other matters raised by plaintiff call for comment.

Plaintiff complains of the exclusion by the trial court of a communication to her from a patent examiner in relation to a pending application by plaintiff for a patent on the subject matter of the invention here involved. Disregarding questions as to the hearsay nature of the document, this was not a final action or determination of the agency itself, and, in our judgment, any inferences as to patentability of either the process or the new use based thereon would be most speculative, to say the least. There was no prejudicial error in its exclusion.

Plaintiff also charges error in the denial of her offer of the testimony of an expert witness who testified on her behalf in the previous litigation between the parties as to the patentability of the process. The witness was said to be out of the jurisdiction. It suffices to dismiss this objection that the subject matter of the respective actions is not substantially identical. *Welch* v. *County of Essex*, 6 N. J. Super. 422 (Cty. Ct. 1949), affirmed, 6 N. J. Super. 184 (App. Div. 1950). In fact, it is substantially different.

It is argued that there was error in not instructing the jury to take into consideration certain facets of the evidence in relation to the good faith of the defendants, *e.g.*, Kell's failure to consult with plaintiff on the facts before arriving at the opinion of Oroshnik's inventorship, etc. But the trial court has broad discretion in referring to specific evidence in the course of his charge. There was no prejudicial mistake in exercising such discretion here.

Criticism is voiced by plaintiff of the court's charge in relation to the willfulness, malice, or good faith attendant

Appendix C—

*Opinion of the Superior Court of New Jersey,
Appellate Division.*

upon defendants' acts. Basically, subject to the following comments, the charge was in our judgment correct. At one point, however, in relation to the liability of Oroshnik in acting upon the advice of Dr. Kell that he was the inventor, the court stated that "if they conspired together" (*i.e.,* Oroshnik and Kell) "he is certainly responsible for it. If it was reasonable, then he is not." Although we find this language neutralized by the charge as a whole, the reference to conspiracy as an antonym to non-actionable conduct in this context was inappropriate and could have been prejudicial.

Furthermore, the court's use of the term "malice" (or malicious) could have been misleading to the jury. In charging a jury in this area that term is best limited to the issue of punitive damages, since its ordinary meaning is spite or ill will, concepts not requisites to liability for general damages in relation to this tort. Legally, "malice" in this field of law means "the intentional doing of a wrongful act without justification or excuse." *Louis Kamm, Inc.* v. *Flink,* 113 N. J. L. 582, 588 (E. & A. 1934); and see *DiCristofaro* v. *Laurel Grove Memorial Park,* 43 N. J. Super, 244, 255-256 (App. Div. 1957). Therefore the jury should be told that it would be wrongful for defendants to specify Oroshnik as inventor on the patent if plaintiff was the inventor and if defendants knew or reasonably should have known that fact. Liability must here be premised upon knowledge, actual or reasonably imputable, since inventorship is a mixed question of law and fact, often reasonably debatable, and the requisite to liability, as indicated, is the "intentional doing" of the wrongful act. Good or bad faith were therefore properly charged here by the trial court as criteria of liability for general damages. But malice, as noted, if mentioned at all, should be expressly confined to the issue of punitive damages. (In other respects the charge as to punitive damages below was essentially correct.)

Plaintiff complains that the trial court refused to instruct the jury that statements in an application by Ortho to the Canadian patent authorities for a patent on the process here involved averring patentability of the process constituted admissions evidential against Ortho. Although the request to charge was not precisely so framed, the general subject matter was covered therein. We think an instruction on the point would have been appropriate although we would not find reversible error in the omission, taken alone, since the pertinent evidence was admitted.

Patentability, as indicated above, is a mixed question of law and fact. Canadian law on patentability is essentially the same as United States law. See Patent Act, 1935, c. 32, §§2(d), 28; see also *Commissioner of Patents v. Ciba Ltd.*, [1959] S. C. R. 378; *Metalliflex Ltd. v. Rodi and Wienenberger*, [1961] S. C. R. 117. Ortho informed the Canadian authorities that notwithstanding the Beilstein reference the patent claim on the process was "clearly in an allowable condition." So far as that statement involved factual elements it was an admission by defendants contradictory to their trial position here. See *Bauman v. Royal Indem. Co.*, 36 N. J. 12 (1961); but see *Simmons Company v. A. Brandwein & Co.*, 250 F. 2d 440, 451-452 (7th Cir. 1957).

VIII.

Plaintiff's last major contention is the alleged unfair and prejudicial handling of the case as a whole by the trial judge against her and in favor of defendants. Detailed discussion of the items of complaint is unnecessary as there is to be a retrial in any event.

Appendix C—

Opinion of the Superior Court of New Jersey,
Appellate Division.

We find no basis whatever for the implication that the trial judge was unfair and biased against plaintiff in his trial conduct. However, his demeanor during the trial may, perhaps, have unconsciously reflected his opinion, frankly expressed at the hearing of the plaintiff's motion for a new trial, that this action was "nothing but a continuation of a process of annoying the defendants because of the irritation of the plaintiff because of her discharge." Notwithstanding that private view, and our disagreement with some of his rulings, we think the trial judge endeavored conscientiously to discharge his duties in this difficult assignment with fairness and in accordance with the law. Much of the difficulty here lay in plaintiff's frequent refusal to accept trial rulings without extended argument, possibly due to her lack of experience in the conduct of a trial and her handicapped position as both attorney *pro se* and sole witness for her side of the case.

Miscellaneous additional points raised by plaintiff have been examined and found either without merit or inconsequential.

Reversed and remanded for a new trial as to defendants Ortho, Oroshnik, and Johnson & Johnson.

APPENDIX D

Constitution, Statutes, Rules of the United States Patent Office and Excerpts from the Manual of Patent Examining Procedure, U.S. Department of Commerce (1961).

United States Constitution

Art. I Sec. 8 Clause 8

Congress shall have Power to promote the Progress of Science and useful Arts by securing to Authors and Inventors the exclusive Right to their respective Writings and Discoveries.

Art. VI

* * * This Constitution, and the Laws of the United States which shall be made in Pursuance thereof; and all Treaties made, or which shall be made, under the Authority of the United States, shall be the supreme Law of the Land; and the Judges in every state shall be bound thereby, any Thing in the Constitution or Laws of any State to the Contrary notwithstanding. * * *

28 U.S.C. 1257 (1)

Final judgments or decrees rendered by the highest court of a state in which a decision could be had, may be reviewed by the Supreme Court as follows:

(1) By appeal, where is drawn in question the validity of a treaty or statute of the United States and the decision is against its validity.

Appendix D—Constitution, Statutes, Rules, etc.

28 U.S.C. 2103

If an appeal to the Supreme Court is improvidently taken from the decision of the highest court of a state, or of a United States Court of Appeals, in a case where the proper mode of a review is by petition for certiorari, this alone shall not be ground for dismissal; but the papers whereon the appeal was taken shall be regarded and acted on as a petition for writ of certiorari and as if duly presented to the Supreme Court at the time the appeal was taken. * * *

§2403. Intervention by United States; constitutional question

In any action, suit or proceeding in a court of the United States to which the United States or any agency, officer or employee thereof is not a party, wherein the constitutionality of any Act of Congress affecting the public interest is drawn in question, the court shall certify such fact to the Attorney General, and shall permit the United States to intervene for presentation of evidence, if evidence is otherwise admissible in the case, and for argument on the question of constitutionality. The United States shall, subject to the applicable provisions of law, have all the rights of a party and be subject to all liabilities of a party as to court costs to the extent necessary for a proper presentation of the facts and law relating to the question of constitutionality.

35 U.S.C. 101. Inventions patentable

Whoever invents or discovers any new and useful

process, machine, manufacture, or composition of matter, or any new and useful improvement thereof, may obtain a patent therefor, subject to the conditions and requirement of this title.

35 U.S.C. 102. Loss of right to patent

A person shall be entitled to a patent unless * * *

(c) he has abandoned the invention * * *

35 U.S.C. 111. Application for patent

Application for patent shall be made by the inventor * * *

35 U.S.C. 112. Specification

The specification shall contain a written description of the invention, and of the manner and process of making and using it, in such full, clear, concise, and exact terms as to enable any person skilled in the art to which it pertains, or with which it is most nearly connected, to make and use the same, and shall set forth the best mode contemplated by the inventor of carrying out his invention.

The specification shall conclude with one or more claims particularly pointing out and distinctly claiming the subject matter which the applicant regards as his invention. * * *

35 U.S.C. 115. Oath of applicant

The applicant shall make oath that he believes

himself to be the original and first inventor of the process, machine, manufacture, or composition of matter, or improvement thereof, for which he solicits a patent; and shall state of what country he is a citizen. * * *

35 U.S.C. 135. Interferences

Whenever an application is made for a patent which, in the opinion of the Commissioner, would interfere with any pending application, or with any unexpired patent, he shall give notice thereof to the applicants, or applicant and patentee, as the case may be. The question of priority of invention shall be determined by a board of patent interferences (consisting of three examiners of interferences) whose decision, if adverse to the claim of an applicant, shall constitute the final refusal by the Patent Office of the claims involved, and the Commissioner may issue a patent to the applicant who is adjudged the prior inventor. A final judgment adverse to a patentee from which no appeal or other review has been or can be taken or had shall constitute cancellation of the claims involved from the patent, and notice thereof shall be endorsed on copies of the patent thereafter distributed by the Patent Office.

A claim which is the same as, or for the same or substantially the same subject matter as, a claim of an issued patent may not be made in any application unless such a claim is made prior to one year from the date on which the patent was granted.

Appendix D—Constitution, Statutes, Rules, etc.

35 U.S.C. 154. Contents and term of patent

Every patent shall contain a short title of the invention and a grant to the patentee, his heirs or assigns, for the term of seventeen years, of the right to exclude others from making, using, or selling the invention throughout the United States, referring to the specification for the particulars thereof. A copy of the specification and drawings shall be annexed to the patent and be a part thereof.

35 U.S.C. 251. Reissue of defective patents

Whenever any patent is, through error without any deceptive intention, deemed wholly or partly inoperative or invalid, by reason of a defective specification or drawing, or by reason of the patentee claiming more or less than he had a right to claim in the patent, the Commissioner shall, on the surrender of such patent and the payment of the fee required by law, reissue the patent for the invention disclosed in the original patent, and in accordance with a new and amended application, for the unexpired part of the term of the original patent. No new matter shall be introduced into the application for reissue.

35 U.S.C. 253. Disclaimer

Whenever, without any deceptive intention, a claim of a patent is invalid the remaining claims shall not thereby be rendered invalid. A patentee, whether of the whole or any sectional interest therein, may, on payment of the fee required by law, make disclaimer of any complete claim, stating therein the extent of his interest in such patent. Such disclaimer shall be in writing and recorded in the Patent Office; and it shall thereafter be considered as part of the original patent to the extent of the interest possessed by the disclaimant and by those claiming under him.

Rules of the United States Patent Office

37 C.F.R. 1.41

Applicant for patent. (a) a patent must be applied for and the application papers must be signed and the necessary oath executed by the actual inventor in all cases, * * *

37 C.F.R. 1.205

Interference with a patent; copying claims from patent.

(a) Before an interference will be declared with a patent, the applicant must present in his application, copies of all the claims of the patent which also define his invention and such claims must be patentable in the application...

37 C.F.R. 1.216 (a) (4)

...the preliminary statement must set forth the following facts relating to conception of the invention: * * *

(4) The date of the first act or acts susceptible of proof...which, if proven, would establish conception of the invention, and a brief description of such act or acts; if there have been no such acts, it must be so stated. * * *

Appendix D—Constitution, Statutes, Rules, etc.

Manual of Patent Examining Procedure U.S. Department of Commerce (1961)

Sec. 706.03 (k) Duplicate Claims

Inasmuch as a patent is supposed to be limited to only one invention , or at most, several closely related indivisible inventions, limiting an application to a single claim, or a single claim to each of the related inventions might appear to be logical as well as convenient. However, court decisions have confirmed applicant's right to restate (i.e., by plural claiming) his invention in a reasonable number of ways. * * *

Sec. 806.05 (f)

A process and a product made by the process can be shown to be distinct inventions if ... the product as claimed can be made by another and materially different process.

Sec. 1102.01 (b):

* * * when an interference is declared involving a patentee and the Examiner is of the opinion that the application or applications contain claims not patentably different from the issue of the interference, he should append to the letter to the applicant a statement that such claims, specifying them by number, will be held subject to the decision in the interference. The reason for making such statement applies equally well to an interference involving only applications. * * *

IN THE

Supreme Court of the United States

OCTOBER TERM, 1965.

No. 595

FERNANDA MISANI,

Appellant,

vs.

ORTHO PHARMACEUTICAL CORP., a New Jersey corporation, JOHNSON & JOHNSON, a New Jersey corporation, ROBERT W. JOHNSON, HARRY C. McKENZIE, BERTON J. TODD, EVAN R. SPALT, JOHN FRIEBELY and WILLIAM OROSHNIK,

Appellees.

MOTION TO DISMISS.

CLYDE A. SZUCH,
PITNEY, HARDIN & KIPP,
    Attorneys for Appellees other than
      Johnson & Johnson and Robert W. Johnson,
      570 Broad Street,
          Newark, New Jersey 07102.
STANLEY C. SMOYER,
    Attorney for Appellees,
      Johnson & Johnson and Robert W. Johnson,
      501 George Street,
          New Brunswick, New Jersey.

TABLE OF CONTENTS.

TABLE OF CASES.

OTHER AUTHORITIES.

Supreme Court of the United States

OCTOBER TERM, 1965

No. ⋯⋯⋯⋯⋯

FERNANDA MISANI,

Appellant,

vs.

ORTHO PHARMACEUTICAL CORP., a New Jersey
Corporation, *et als.,*

Appellees.

MOTION TO DISMISS.

Appellees, pursuant to Rule 16 of the Revised Rules of
the Supreme Court of the United States, move to dismiss
the above appeal on the grounds that (a) it does not present
a substantial federal question; (b) the alleged federal questions advanced by appellant were either not properly raised
or passed upon below; and (c) the final judgment of the
New Jersey Supreme Court rests on an adequate non-federal basis.

Statement of Case.

This is an action by a discharged employee against her former employer, Ortho Pharmaceutical Corp. (hereinafter called "Ortho"), the employer's parent corporation, Johnson & Johnson, the Chairman of the Board of Johnson & Johnson, Robert W. Johnson and five individuals who were officers or supervisory employees of Ortho at the time of plaintiff's discharge—Harry C. McKenzie, President, Evan R. Spalt, Vice President, Berton J. Todd, Vice President, John Friebely, Director of Personnel and William Oroshnik, Director of the Organic Research Division and plaintiff's supervisor.*

This suit stems from the fact that Ortho Pharmaceutical Corp., obtained a United States patent, 2,878,263, and applied for a Canadian patent on a chemical compound, 4-methyl-4-phenyl-5-pyrazolone (hereinafter called "the compound"). Appellant's causes of action as set out in her complaint and as reflected in the pretrial order are that appellees (1) wrongfully, maliciously and fraudulently deprived her of credit by failing to designate her the inventor in the United States patent application and issued patent (P1a to P11a-11; P31a-14 to 21),** which application and patent designated William Oroshnik the inventor of the compound; (2) maliciously committed errors in the specifications and claim of the patent application (P11a-12 to P12a-15; P32a-16; (3) failed to claim the process of making the compound in the patent application (P11a-12 to

---

* Since plaintiff's discharge, Messrs. McKenzie and Todd have died and Dr. Oroshnik has resigned his position at Ortho.

** References to the appendix filed with appellant's Jurisdictional Statement are cited "Pj(page)a". References to appellees' and appellant's respective appendices filed in the Appellate Division are cited as "D(page)a" and "P(page)a".

P12a-15; P32a-14 to 16); (4) breached her contract of employment with Ortho and invention assignment agreement by failing to give her credit as the inventor (P12a-19 to P14a-8; P31a-19 to 20); (5) wrongfully applied for the patent before the invention had been fully developed and exploited (P15a-10 to P16a-14; P32a-18 to 22); and (6) wrongfully applied for a Canadian patent (P37a-10 to 23). For all of these wrongs, appellant sought compensatory and punitive damages, and an adjudication that she was the inventor of the compound and its process of manufacture and that the appellees had no property rights in the patent or the compound. P1a to P16a; P34a-16 to 17; P37a-17 to 23.

Appellant commenced her employment with Ortho on January 10, 1955. D11a-15 to 17. Her employment resulted from her response to an advertisement for an organic chemist to do ''research in synthetic medicinal chemistry'', the work to be of ''basic character.'' DEx. D-1; D76a; D11a-23 to 28. During the period of her employment by Ortho, appellant's work involved basic research and her efforts were directed toward making new medicinal compounds. D12a-14 to D13a-19.

Appellant's employment terminated in April, 1956 (D11a-18 to 22) when she was discharged by Oroshnik, her supervisor. As a result of her discharge, appellant instituted suit against these same appellees in another state court proceeding in which she sought damages, *inter alia*, for the discharge, which was alleged to be wrongful, and for libel and slander. App. Div. Docket No. A-711-60. The trial court dismissed that suit at the close of appellant's case. The Appellate Division of the Superior Court affirmed the dismissal and the New Jersey Supreme Court denied appellant's petition for certification. 38 N. J. 304

(1962). Thereafter, this Court denied a Petition for Writ of Certiorari. 372 U. S. 959 (1963).

During the course of the trial of the instant case, appellant testified to having invented the compound and the process for its preparation. P107a to P108a-23; P110a-8 to 11; P114a-3 to 20; D7a-36 to 39. This testimony was sharply disputed by Oroshnik, the person designated in the patent on the compound as its inventor. Oroshnik's testimony was that he, not appellant, conceived the idea for the compound, that he had disclosed the idea to appellant, told her how to make it but left to her the details of the process for its synthesis. D34a-5 to 7; D35a-5 to 28; D37a-29 to 32; P131a-15 to P133a-6. He further testified that when he told the appellant to make the compound, he knew it could be achieved because chemical theory predicted it. D37a-29 to 32.

Oroshnik also testified that he told Dr. Robert W. Kell, a Johnson & Johnson staff patent attorney who evaluated the compound for patenting, that he had conceived the idea for the compound and had directed the appellant to make it (P133a-11 to 13). However, Oroshnik did not tell Kell he was the inventor (P133a-14 to 16) or that he had invented the process for making the compound (P133a-17 to 19).

Kell testified it was his conclusion that Oroshnik was the inventor of the compound and described in detail the factual and legal basis for his decision. D52a-32 to 36; D49a-22 to D51a-30.

Appellees introduced the testimony of Roger T. McLean, Esq., a qualified expert in the field of patent law (D58a-28 to D59a-16), to show the patent on the compound to be invalid. He testified that a reference in a German chemical encyclopedia completely invalidated the patent (D59a-22 to 42). Earlier in the trial, appellant admitted the invalidity of the patent (D51a-32 to 35), but asserted it could be made valid by adding an use description to it (P123a-13 to 22). McLean disputed this and stated that no amount of amendment could validate a patent on the compound itself. D60a-2 to 24. McLean also testified that if Oroshnik conceived the idea for the compound as he testified (P132a-20 to 25), he would be the inventor even if he did not do the actual bench work (D67a-5 to 25).

Appellant testified that she had invented the process for making the compound. D7a-36 to 40. McLean was specifically directed to the appellant's testimonial description of the process for making the compound (D60a25 to D61a-25) and was asked to render his opinion as to whether the process was novel and patentable. He stated the process was neither novel nor patentable. D61a-31 to D66a-38. Kell also stated the process to be unpatentable. D53a-10 to 12.*

No proof was adduced on the subject of the use to which the compound could be put, and indeed, there was nothing stated prior to or during the trial which would have indicated that the use of the compound or any claim for the discovery of such use was an issue in this case.

At the close of appellant's case, the suit was dismissed against Messrs. McKenzie, Spalt, Todd, Friebely and Johnson for failure to produce any evidence connecting them with the patenting of the compound. D25a-6 to 18. The suit against Oroshnik, Ortho and Johnson & Johnson was submitted to the jury, which returned an unanimous verdict for no cause of action. After a denial of appellant's application for a new trial and her unsuccessful direct petition for certification to the New Jersey Supreme

---

* Since the start of this action, appellant has secured a patent on the process but that patent is not part of the record. Pj31a.

Court, the matter was briefed and argued before the Appellate Division of the Superior Court.

The Appellate Division unanimously affirmed the dismissal of the case at the close of appellants' proofs as to five appellees but reversed the trial court judgment as to Oroshnik and the two corporate appellees and remanded the case for retrial as to them. In reaching this result, the Appellate Division agreed that the issued patent on the compound was invalid (Pj18a), that the compound itself could not be validly patented (*Ibid.*), and consequently that appellant was not denied any actionable inventorship credit on the compound (Pj19a). However, the Court held appellant could have been wrongfully denied inventorship credit for the process of making the compound and, although it was never at issue in this case, for the use to which the compound could be put. This holding was premised on the Court's conclusion that the designation of Oroshnik as the inventor in the issued patent, which only formally claimed the compound as the invention, was also a "representation" that Oroshnik was the inventor of the process and use which were described in the specification of the patent.

The parties cross-petitioned for certification to the New Jersey Supreme Court which Court granted the cross-petitions. The Supreme Court affirmed the lower court decisions as to McKenzie, Spalt, Todd, Friebely and Johnson. It reversed the Appellate Division's holding as to the remaining appellees and reinstated the jury verdict of no cause of action. In reaching this latter conclusion, the Court held (a) the jury verdict to mean that Oroshnik and not appellant conceived the idea for the compound, (b) that by reason of an assignment agreement she had executed appellant had transferred her property rights to discoveries she made while employed by Ortho to it and (c) that there was no misrepresentation as to inventorship of the process for making the compound and its use, and, in any event, it would not recognize a cause of action for such misrepresentation when the basis therefor was factually grounded on implications from a patent limited in its claim to the compound in question which patent was conceded by all to be invalid. Pj3a to Pj8a.

ARGUMENT.

Appellant has failed to establish any basis for this appeal.

At pages 9 to 11 of her jurisdictional statement, appellant presents eight questions allegedly presented by this case. Although not all of these questions are discussed by appellant in part F of her jurisdictional statement, appellees shall comment upon each question.

The initial question raised and argued by appellant involves a claim of patent misuse by reason of an alleged possible extension of monopoly. This is said to be a question because of the issuance of two patents to appellant, 3,079,397 and 3,166,475, since the termination of her employment at Ortho and the possibility that Ortho's rights gained through the patent on the compound, U. S. P. 2,878,263, will be extended if plaintiff is compelled to assign those two patents to Ortho. This question has neither been raised before nor decided by any court during the litigation between the parties.

As part of her employment with Ortho, appellant executed an invention assignment agreement whereby she agreed to assign all her rights,

> "in inventions, improvements and ideas which during the period of his [sic] employment, he [sic]

has made or conceived or may make or conceive, either solely or jointly with others, in the course of his [sic] employment. . . ."

The three Courts which have heard this case have held this assignment agreement to be valid and, have further held that by reason of it, appellant transferred to Ortho her property rights in inventions encompassed by the agreement. Indeed, no other conclusion could have been reached in view of the absence of any evidence indicating infirmities in the agreement.

However, no court has held that the two patents issued to appellant are encompassed by the assignment agreement; no court has compelled plaintiff to assign those patents to Ortho; no claim has been made by appellees that these two patents should be assigned to Ortho; and, as noted in the Appellate Division opinion, these two patents are not even a part of the record in this case.

Question 2 is in part answered by the answer to the previous question. As noted, the invention assignment agreement vested Ortho with all of plaintiff's property rights in inventions made by her while in its employ. As held by all the lower courts, even without this agreement, the result is the same because plaintiff was hired to exercise her inventive faculties for Ortho and, in such case, under settled state and federal law, the inventions belong to the employer. *Kinkade* v. *N. Y. Shipbuilding Corp.*, 21 N. J. 362 (Sup. Ct. 1956); *U. S.* v. *Dubilier Condenser Corp.*, 289 U. S. 178 (1933).

Intertwined in the second question is the assertion that a patent on the compound was secured by Ortho in the name of the non-inventor. Such an assertion does not lie in view of the jury verdict of no cause of action in favor of Oroshnik, Ortho and Johnson & Johnson and the New

Jersey Supreme Court's holding that the proper interpretation of that verdict is that Oroshnik and not the appellant was the inventor of the compound patented by Ortho. Pj5a.

The third question set out by appellant, totally misstates the holding of the New Jersey Supreme Court. In the patent which issued to Ortho, there was a single claim and that was on the compound 4-methyl-4-phenyl-5-pyrazolone. No claim was made for either the process or use although both were set out in the specification portion of the patent as required by 35 U. S. C. §112. In considering the claim on the compound and the balance of the material in the patent, the Court was concerned with the question whether there was any representation made that Oroshnik was the inventor of a patentable process for making the compound and the use to which it could be put. The Supreme Court held, as a matter of fact, that no such representation had been made. Pj6a to Pj8a. That conclusion is supported by the unambiguous language of the patent in general, by the language of the claim in particular, and by the holding of this and other courts in the analogous field of infringement cases where it has been held that the claim alone defines the invention. *Brown* v. *Guild*, 90 U. S. 181 (1874); *Graver Tank & Mfg. Co., Inc.* v. *Linde Air Products Co.*, 336 U. S. 271 (1949), *aff'd. on reh.*, 339 U. S. 605 (1949); *Straussler* v. *United States*, 290 F. 2d 827 (Ct. of Cl. 1961).

Questions 4 and 5 are interrelated and stem apparently from the fact that Ortho has not disclaimed the patent on the compound. The patent is invalid and, as noted by the lower courts, appellant has steadfastly conceded the invalidity. Pj4a to Pj5a. 35 U. S. C. §253 provides that a patentee "... may, on payment of the fee required by law, make disclaimer of any complete claim . . .". This statute is permissive and neither its language nor the cases interpreting it have imposed a duty upon the patentee to disclaim. See, *United Carbon Co., Inc.* v. *Carbon Black Research Foundation,* 59 F. Supp. 384, 388 (D. Md. 1945). In addition, because Ortho was vested with the full property rights in the patent in question and in inventions of appellant made while in its employ, the state courts correctly held it was under no obligation to correct alleged errors in the patent on the compound or to disclaim.

In question six, appellant questions whether a patentee who has not disclaimed may nonetheless assert the invalidity of his patent. In this case, invalidity was an issue because it bore directly on plaintiff's asserted right to credit and the amount of damage, if any, she sustained. As stated by the Appellate Division, the issue of patent invalidity was tried with plaintiff's acquiescence. Pj33a. Additionally to be noted is the principle that the doctrine of estoppel has no application to a case, such as the instant one, where it has been shown and the jury must have found that the patentee acted in good faith in securing the patent. *Greenwood* v. *Bracher,* 1 Fed. 856, 858 (Cir. Ct. D. N. J. 1880).

Question 7 challenges the fact that the state courts did not follow the procedural rules of the United States Patent Office and appellant asserts thereby a violation of the Supremacy Clause of the United States Constitution. The Patent Office procedural rule which appellant asserts was not followed would prohibit a party in an interference proceeding from testifying as to his conception without extrinsic corroborating evidence. In addition to the fact that state courts are not required to follow the rules of procedure of federal administrative agencies, the rule contended for by appellant would in no event have had application to the present case. Where, as here, there are two competing parties, each alleging he is the inventor and claiming to have disclosed the invention to the other, the issue of invention "is really only one of veracity" and there "are no presumptions or artificial rules regulating such an investigation, and the evidence of one witness may be sufficient." *C. F. Mueller Co.* v. *Zeregas Sons, Consol.,* 12 F. 2d 517, 518 (2nd Cir. 1926); *followed, Concrete Mixing & Conveying Co.* v. *R. C. Storrie & Co.,* 27 F. 2d 838, 840 (9th Cir. 1928), *affirmed,* 282 U. S. 175 (1930).

The final question raised by appellant is whether her contract of employment with Ortho, as interpreted by the state courts, is "unconstitutional" and whether the application of the doctrine of *res judicata* denied due process to appellant. Appellant has, throughout this second suit, attempted to relitigate the issues raised and determined in the first suit. Among those issues was the validity of appellant's contract of employment and the propriety of appellees' actions in discharging appellant from Ortho's employ. Those issues were determined favorably to appellees and, in this case, all the courts, under normally accepted rules of *res judicata,* have prevented appellant from relitigating these issues.

In the instant case, appellant contended that the assignment agreement she executed was invalid because the employment contract was not for a fixed term and therefor not supported by adequate consideration. That legal contention was rejected by the lower courts (*Patent and Licensing Corp.* v. *Olsen,* 188 F. 2d 522 (2nd Cir. 1951); *Goodyear Tire & Rubber Co.* v. *Miller,* 22 F. 2d 353 (9th Cir. 1927)) and no constitutional question was involved.

Conclusion.

For the foregoing reasons, it is submitted that there are no substantial federal questions presented, that the judgment of the New Jersey Supreme Court rests on an adequate non-federal basis and that this Court should grant this motion to dismiss.

Respectfully submitted,

CLYDE A. SZUCH,
PITNEY, HARDIN & KIPP,
Attorneys for Appellees other than Johnson
& Johnson and Robert W. Johnson,
570 Broad Street,
Newark 2, New Jersey.

STANLEY C. SMOYER,
Attorney for Appellees Johnson & Johnson
and Robert W. Johnson,
501 George Street,
New Brunswick, New Jersey.

Dated: October 22, 1965.

In The

Supreme Court of the United States

October Term, 1965

Docket No. 595

FERNANDA MISANI,

Plaintiff-Appellant,

v.

ORTHO PHARMACEUTICAL CORPORATION, a New Jersey corporation, JOHNSON & JOHNSON, a New Jersey corporation, ROBERT W. JOHNSON, HARRY C. McKENZIE, BERTON J. TODD, EVAN R. SPALT, JOHN FRIEBELY and WILLIAM OROSHNIK,

Defendants-Appellees.

ON APPEAL FROM THE SUPREME COURT OF NEW JERSEY

APPELLANT'S BRIEF IN OPPOSITION TO MOTION TO DISMISS

FERNANDA MISANI,

Plaintiff-Appellant Pro Se,
40 Tamaques Way,
Westfield, New Jersey

Martin Lutz Appellate Printers, Inc.
New York ● Philadelphia ● Newark ● New Brunswick

INDEX

Page

Table of Citations

Index

U.S. CONSTITUTION CITED

STATUTES CITED:

Index

SUPREME COURT OF THE UNITED STATES

October Term 1965

Docket No. 595

FERNANDA MISANI,

Plaintiff-Appellant,

v.

ORTHO PHARMACEUTICAL CORPORATION, a New Jersey
corporation, JOHNSON & JOHNSON, a New Jersey corporation, ROBERT W. JOHNSON, HARRY C. McKENZIE,
BERTON J. TODD, EVAN R. SPALT, JOHN FRIEBELY
and WILLIAM OROSHNIK,

Defendants-Appellees.

ON APPEAL FROM THE SUPREME COURT OF NEW JERSEY

APPELLANT'S BRIEF IN OPPOSITION TO MOTION TO DISMISS

INTRODUCTION*

Compelling reasons for denying the motion to dismiss the appeal appear on the face of appellees' brief.**

---

*   On November 1, 1965, the appellant was admitted to the New Jersey Bar.

**   Appellant's Jurisdictional Statement and appellees' brief are cited herein as "PJ (page)" and "D.Br. (page)" respectively. References to appellant's and appellees' respective appendixes filed in the New Jersey proceedings are cited as "R (page) a" and "D (page) a". The appendixes annexed to the Jurisdictional Statement are cited as Appendix A, B, C and D respectively. The appendix annexed hereto is cited as Appendix E.

ARGUMENT

I. Federal Supremacy in the Patent Field.

In support of their contention that the judgment below should be sustained because it rests on an adequate non-federal basis (D.Br.1), appellees rely on two arguments: 1) that the New Jersey courts have held the contract* valid and enforceable against the plaintiff (D.Br.8), and 2) that the jury returned a general verdict of no cause of action (D.Br.6).

Both arguments are untenable. This Court has held that, in matters involving federal policy, the federal law is supreme and state courts must yield. Sperry v. Florida, 373 U.S. 379. A state may not extend the life of a patent, under the guise of enforcing a contract. Sears, Roebuck & Co. v. Stiffel Company, 376 U.S. 225, 231; Brulotte v. Thys, 379 U.S. 29.

In this case, the federal patent laws invalidate a compulsory contract prepared by the legal staff of Johnson & Johnson, for the benefit of the parent company and some eighty subsidiaries, where the contract extends the monopoly for the employer, beyond the seventeen-year period. 35 U.S.C. 154; Mercoid Corp. v. Mid-Continent Invest. Co., 320 U.S. 661. (PJ 6, 13, 22-28). The judgment of the Supreme Court of New Jersey cannot be sustained, inasmuch as the federal questions involved in this appeal were timely raised and argued before the New Jersey courts. The Certificate of Federal Questions annexed hereto (Appendix E), so states.

---

* The full text of the contract is shown at page 8 of Appellant's Petition for Certiorari, Docket No. 819, Fall Term 1962, nine copies of which have been submitted.

II. The Judgment of the Supreme Court of New Jersey does not Rest on an adequate Non-Federal Ground, but is an Explicit Determination of the Federal Questions, and Invalidates Federal Law.

The Supreme Court of New Jersey, in deciding this case in favor of all the appellees, has 1) assumed that Oroshnik conceived the idea and 2) has held that conception of idea is sufficient to constitute inventorship (Appendix B,5a).

Taking the matters in the reverse order, it is submitted that this is an unconstitutional substitution of a state standard in a field of federal pre-emption. Under federal law, 35 U.S.C. 101, 112 and 154, inventorship of a compound requires three elements: a) conception of idea b) reduction to practice and c) a showing of utility. (Compare appellant's Request to charge the jury at R39a to R41a; Exception to the charge, R75a-8 and Appendix C at 19a).

In conclusion, the Supreme Court of New Jersey has not based its decision on a non-federal ground, but has expressly passed upon the federal question, and decided it in a manner which invalidates federal law.

III. The General Verdict of No Cause of Action is the Result of the Errors in the Court's Charge, as to the Applicable Federal Law.

On the factual issue of "Who conceived the idea?", the Supreme Court of New Jersey has inferred that the jury found in Oroshnik's favor. It summarily said:

> "...in the light of the whole record including the trial court's charge, we believe

that the jury's verdict may fairly be read
as evidencing its finding that there had
been no lack of good faith...and that, as between the plaintiff and Oroshnik, the latter
rather than the former, conceived the idea
for the compound" (Appendix B, 5a).

It is this bare inference, not supported by a single
reference to the record, or to the court's charge,
which, according to the appellees, constitutes an
independent non-federal ground for sustaining the
judgment below (D.Br.6,8).

The Appellate Division, however, reversing in
favor of appellant, had found substantial errors in
the court's charge to the jury. The most flagrant
errors are:

1. The judge charged that the Beilstein reference
   amounted to a prior invention and said:

   "We know she (appellant) was not the first
   inventor..." (R57a).

The Appellate Division found the instruction erroneous and contrary to 35 U.S.C. 112. The
Beilstein reference, (R282a), merely a "type
formula", could not constitute an invention. It
lacked the reduction to practice and showing of
utility (Appendix C, 19a to 20a; 28a, 31a).

The judge also charged that the patent, U. S. P.
2,878,263, was "invalid, no good" (R55a) and
appellant could not be deprived of credit for
something worthless.

2. The judge charged that the error, the too broad claim of U.S.P. 2,878,263, could not be corrected. He said:

> "...Dr. Misani has repeatedly pressed the idea that Ortho could get a good patent if they changed the wording of the claim; and we have had evidence that they couldn't" (R68a).

On the other hand, the Appellate Division found that, under the new statutory provisions, 35 U.S.C. 100(b), the error could be corrected, and that the judge failed to instruct the jury on the applicable federal law, with respect to the reissue provisions for correcting errors in a patent. 35 U.S.C. 251. (Appendix C, 20a to 21a and footnote; 27a, 28a).

3. The judge also charged:

> "It does not make any difference whether they (appellees) could, or whether they couldn't (correct the error)...that's none of her business (R68a)...They don't have to correct the patent" (R66a).

4. The judge charged:

> An employer may "throw inventions of an employee out of the window" (R66a).

5. The judge said:

> "...As far as that process is concerned, frankly, I don't see anything in it at all ..." (R67a).

The Appellate Division, reversing, found error in the failure "to make such minimal exposition of the applicable law" (Appendix C, 22a to 27a) as to the standards of patentability of a process.

6. Appellant requested the trial judge to submit the following interrogatories to the jury:

    1. Who conceived the idea?

    2. Who reduced the idea to practice?

    3. Who devised the means of reducing the idea to practice?

    4. Have the defendants proved that Oroshnik actually conceived, supervised and directed the project, except for bare fact that the plaintiff, a senior chemist, worked in the department?

    Manifestly, the interrogatories were framed to elicit fact-findings in accordance with federal law in a pre-empted field. The trial judge refused to submit the interrogatories to the jury (R213a; R75a-27). The Appellate Division properly found error in the denial (Appendix C, 31a footnote).

7. The judge did not submit the facts to the jury, but essentially charged that Oroshnik was the inventor, because he was in the rank of supervisor. He said:

    "On that point, this is the law: ..a presumption arises that (he) is the inventor (R62a)...Many people invent things but don't even know how to make them" (R63a).

The judge refused to charge the jury to consider appellant's expertise in the field of the invention, (PJ 32) and Oroshnik's admitted lack of familiarity with the subject matter (R26a-16).

8. The judge never submitted the issue of appellees' good faith or bad faith to the jury. On the contrary, he essentially charged that respondent Oroshnik was in good faith because Kell, a member of the patent staff of Johnson & Johnson, concluded that he was "the legal inventor" (R60a; R64a), and that Kell was in good faith. "That's what he had to deal with" (R77a to R78a).

No instruction was given with respect to the duty of a patent attorney to secure a patent in the name of the real inventor. (Compare appellant's Request to Charge, R43a to R47a).

9. The Appellate Division found error in the burden of proof imposed on the appellant. She could not recover for negligence. She should have proved that Kell "acted maliciously, wilfully and wrongfully" and that Oroshnik and Kell "conspired together" (R69a to R71a; Appendix C at 39a).

On the basis of the substantial errors of law, the Appellate Division concluded that the general jury verdict of no cause of action could very well mean nominal damages (Appendix C, 30a), and remanded for trial because appellant could be entitled to punitive damages (Appendix C at 39a).

IV. The Holding of the Trial Judge, that a Scientist has no Right to have his Name on a Patent, is against Public Policy and Invalidates 35 U.S.C. 102(f) and 111.

The trial judge, at the beginning of trial, ruled against the plaintiff on the matter of ownership and held that she had no cause of action for deprivation of intellectual credit (R99a to R101a; R118a). He said:

> "you prove...not that you merely invented it, but that you own it" (R115a to R116a).

Plaintiff's motion for judgment was denied with the language:

> "The Court: The motion of Dr. Misani for a directed verdict is denied...I doubt seriously whether there is a legal right to be presented to the jury...Such examination of the law as I have made indicates to me that there is no right in the law for a person who has no property rights in an invention, to insist upon his or her name being mentioned" (R199a; pp. 782-785 of transcript).

The Appellate Division, in reversing in favor of appellant, had properly found that the holding of the trial judge invalidates 35 U.S.C. 102(f) and is against public policy. A patent must issue in the name of the inventor (Appendix C at 16a). The Appellate Division also noted the prejudice in the "pervasive undertone in the charge as a whole of lack of merit in the plaintiff's entire claim" (Appendix C at 31a).

V. The Supreme Court of New Jersey has issued the Certificate of Federal Questions. The Questions have been timely raised before the Courts below and are Substantial.

On November 1, 1965, the Supreme Court of New Jersey issued the Certificate of Federal Questions (Appendix E, annexed hereto), acknowledging that the federal questions involved in this appeal have been urged and argued by the appellant. Appellees' contention that the questions were not raised below. (D.Br.1,7), is now moot. Further, the New Jersey courts have expressly passed on the federal questions involved.

The following arguments are set forth in answer to appellees' contentions, question per question.

Question 1: Appellees do not deny that assignment of the two patents, U.S.P. 3,079,397 and U.S.P. 3,166,475, would operate to extend the monopoly beyond the seventeen-year period (PJ 6; PJ 22), nor do they deny that the two patents were issued by the United States Patent Office, because an interference proceeding had been instituted and a conflicting interest between the parties had been established. 35 U.S.C. 135 (PJ 5; PJ 11). The rule against double patenting has been consistently applied, since 1819, Odiorne v. Amesbury Natl. Factory, 2 Mason 28; 18 Fed. Cases 578 (No. 10, 430) (C.C.D. Mass. 1819).

Appellees, however, argue that the two patents were not part of the record (D.Br.7). This argument is untenable. During trial, in 1962, appellant offered in evidence a communication from the United States Patent Office, which showed that the two patents would issue (R209a; R185a to R189a; R198a; Appendix C at 38a). The trial judge excluded it. The two patents issued after trial, in 1963 and 1965 respectively, that is, during the pendency of the appeal before the Appellate Division and the New Jersey Supreme Court. Appellant immediately brought the issuance of the two patents to the attention of the courts below, and they are referred to in the courts' opinions (Appendix C at 31-32; Appendix B at 5a).

The question of extension of the monopoly, in conflict with 35 U.S.C. 154, has been raised and argued as soon as the patents issued. The courts below have expressly passed on it with the holding "It is frivolous". Appellees will "presumably compel assignment" of the patents (Appendix C at 15a, 32a, Appendix B at 3a).

Question 2: This question, whether an employer may conceal and "scrap" inventions of an employee, and later, secure a patent in the name of one who is not the inventor, (PJ 4, 7, 29, 32-34), is essentially by-passed by the appellees. Their silence is an implied admission that they concealed and suppressed the invention, in 1956, for malicious motives.

The crux of the matter is that Johnson & Johnson has argued before the courts below that an employer may conceal or abandon inventions of an employee, has no duty to determine who is the inventor and is free to take inventions of one employee and include them in a patent in the name of another employee. The present holding of the New Jersey courts that an employer may "scrap inventions of employees at its unfettered will" (Appendix B at 3a; Appendix C at 14a), under the guise of enforcing proprietary rights, under state law, effectively destroys our constitutional policy. U.S. Const., Art. I, Sec. 8,

C1. 8, and invalidates 35 U.S.C. 102(c). The primary purpose of granting monopolies is to promote the progress of science and useful arts. The inventor himself, or anyone claiming under him, has no right, without just cause or reason, to conceal his invention. Concealment and suppression cause a forfeiture of the right to a patent. Mason v. Hepburn, 13 App. D.C. 86 (D.C. Cir. 1898).

Appellees' motion to dismiss should be denied, to define the scope of federal supremacy and to preserve the constitutional policy of promoting the progress of science and useful arts. The issue is of profound importance in a society where thousands of scientists are employed by large corporations, subject to adhesion-type, "take-it-or-leave-it" contracts.

Question 3: Appellees do not deny that product, process and use in this case constitute a single invention, and concede (D.Br.9) that 35 U.S.C. 112 requires:

> "...a description of the invention, and of the manner and process of making and using it, in such full, clear, concise and exact terms as to enable any person skilled in the art to which it pertains,...to make and use the same and...the best mode contemplated by the inventor of carrying out his invention."

There is no invention until the idea is reduced to practice and utility is shown. Even assuming, arguendo, Oroshnik conceived the idea of making the compound, he could not be the inventor. When he executed the oath that he was the inventor, 35 U.S.C. 115, he knowingly executed a false oath (PJ 28-29).

In direct contrast with appellees' assertion that the issues are not substantial, it should be noted that this Court has recently granted certiorari in Manson v. Brenner, 333 F.2d 234 (C.C.P.A. 1964) cert. granted 33 U.S. Law Week 3349, and in Walker Process Equipment Inc. v. Food Machinery and Chemical Corp., 335 F.2d 315 (7th Cir. 1964) cert. granted 34 U.S. Law Week 3006. These cases involve the identical issues of requirement of utility and fraud on the United States Patent Office in the oath accompanying the application.*

Question 4: is also by-passed (D.Br.9). Appellees do not rebut the facts and the law as presented by the appellant (PJ 11-13; PJ 36).

After U.S.P. 2,878,263 issued, appellant sought an adjudication of inventorship by the United States Patent Office, requested the institution of an interference proceeding and urged that the correction of the too broad claim could be made under the reissue provisions, 35 U.S.C. 251 (R211a; R125a; R198a).

Appellees took advantage of their patentee status and the lack of jurisdiction of the administrative agency over an issued patent. They knew that they would lose in that proceeding and provoked the dissolution of the interference (R210a; R219a). The courts below have ratified Johnson & Johnson's retaining the benefit of the issued patent and refusal to

---

* The cases cited by the appellees at D.Br.9 corroborate appellant's argument. They stand for the rule that claims define the area of the monopoly. The broad claim to the product, in U.S.P.2,878,263, (PJ 15) gave Johnson & Johnson, in 1959, a monopoly for seventeen years, that is, the right of "making, using or selling" the product, by any process and for every use, including the process and use described in the specification. (PJ 23 to 28).

continue the contest to an adjudication of inventorship by the United States Patent Office.

Question 5: is confused with Question 6 (D.Br.9-10).

The nature of a patent, a grant from the government and a monopoly on the public, imposes on a patentee the duty either 1) to correct errors by limiting the broad scope of the claim or claims, 35 U.S.C. 251 or 2) to disclaim the grant. 35 U.S.C. 253 (PJ 12; 36-37). Marconi Wireless Co. v. United States, 320 U.S. 1, 58. This Court in Ensten v. Simon, Asher & Co., 282 U.S. 445, 452, elaborated on the duty of "disavowal of the apparent right to exclude others from something improperly included in the words of the grant".

In conflict with statutory law and the holding of this Court, the courts below have held that an employer may retain a too broad monopoly and has no duty to correct the errors:

> "Ortho owed her no duty...to repair any deficiency in the patent issued, by amendment or otherwise" (Appendix C, at 15a; Appendix B, at 5a).
> "This is none of her business" (R66a).

The case cited by the appellees, United Carbon Co., Inc., v. Carbon Black Research Foundation, 59 F. Supp. 384, 387, 388 (D. Md. 1945), is good authority for the rule that the reissue provisions to correct errors, 35 U.S.C. 251 (formerly Rev. St. Sec. 4916) and the disclaimer provisions, 35 U.S.C. 253 (formerly Rev. St. 4922), are usually in the alternative and not coextensive. What the appellees did in the present case is the opposite: they refused to comply, with neither the reissue nor the disclaimer provisions.

Question 6: Appellees primarily contend that appellant has conceded the invalidity of U.S.P. 2,878,263.* The fact is that appellant never conceded the invalidity of the patent. In reliance on Rule of the United States Patent Office, 37 C.F.R. 1.258, she urged that the trial judge exclude any reference to the defect in the patent (R161a to R163a), requested a charge to the jury to the same effect (R38a), and excepted to the Court's charge (R75a-1 to R75a-13). Her testimony was that the defect, rather than invalidity, could be cured at any time during the seventeen-year period (R123a). The doctrine of estoppel should have been applied against appellees for retaining the full monopoly and refusing to correct the error (PJ 36).

It is significant that the broad product claim of U.S.P. 2,878,263 is now fully valid, under prevaling case law. The recent decisions, Application of Brown, 329 F.2d 1006, 1009 (C.C.P.A. 1964) and E.I. DuPont de Nemours & Co. v. Ladd, 328 F.2d 547 (D.C. Cir. 1964) have held that a mere name and a formula in the prior art do not defeat patentability of a product. It is also significant that, as of this date, no court has ordered the appellees to disclaim U.S.P. 2,878,263 and that they still retain the monopoly under this patent.

Question 7 (PJ 8, 35): Appellees concede that application of the rule of the United States Patent Office, 37 C.F.R. 1.216 (a)(4), would have excluded Oroshnik's testimony (D.Br.10) but seek to deny the jurisdiction of this Court by appeal by claiming that the rules

---

* They state: ..."appellant admitted the invalidity of the patent" (D.Br.4-5)..."the patent was conceded by all to be invalid" (D.Br.7) ..."the issue of patent invalidity was tried with plaintiff's acquiescence" (D.Br.10).

of the United States Patent Office are not binding on state courts. Their contention is in conflict with the holding of this Court, Sperry v. Florida, 373 U.S. 379.

The cases cited by the appellees support appellant's argument, since extrinsic evidence, corroborative of the testimony of each party, was available, "one witness" other than the party, in C.F. Mueller Co. v. Zeregas Sons Consol., 12 F.2d 517, 518 (2nd Cir. 1926) and authentic exhibits in Concrete Mixing & Conveying Co. v. R.C. Storrie & Co., 27 F.2d 838, 840 (9th Cir. 1928).

Question 8: Appellees broadly rely on the doctrine of res judicata, assert that..."the issues were determined favorably to them" and appellant is prevented from relitigating the issues (D.Br.11).

It is submitted that this case is governed by the principle that a prior judgment is res judicata only as to those matters upon the determination of which the finding or verdict was rendered. Mercoid Corp. v. Mid Continent Invest. Co., 320 U.S. 661, 671. The issue determined in the first case was that "the termination of employment was not wrongful ..it being a hiring at will" (Barger, J., first case) at 81a to 82a; 67a; Appendix C at 10a). The contract, now enforced against appellant was not considered in the first case. If the contract of employment was terminable at will and the employer was bound to nothing, the agreement to assign inventions is invalid because totally lacking in mutuality. Further, at the time when appellant urged that the two cases should be consolidated, because of the identical issues on the law and on the facts, appellees opposed consolidation. Application of the doctrine of res judicata rewards appellees for splitting the litigation, and for excluding material evidence in both cases.

CONCLUSION

For the foregoing reasons, it is submitted that this case involves substantial federal questions, that the judgment of the Supreme Court of New Jersey does not rest on an adequate nonfederal ground, and that this Court has jurisdiction, both by appeal and certiorari.

Respectfully submitted,

FERNANDA MISANI
Appellant pro se
40 Tamaques Way
Westfield, New Jersey

APPENDIX E

Certificate of the Supreme Court of New Jersey as to the existence of Federal Questions.

(Filed November 1, 1965)

This matter being open to the Court by the plaintiff-appellant, this Court, in addition to the order made herein, orders it to be certified and made part of the record in this case and of the judgment and entry of affirmance as to the defendants other than Johnson & Johnson, Ortho Pharmaceutical Corporation and William Oroshnik, and entry of judgment of reversal as to defendants Johnson & Johnson, Ortho Pharmaceutical Corporation and William Oroshnik, heretofore rendered and made hereon, that in the oral argument as well as by the briefs and the petition for rehearing made in this Court, plaintiff-appellant urged and relied upon the following questions under the Constitution and the Statutes of the United States:

1. Whether the assignment of U.S.P. 3,079,397 and 3,166,475 from the plaintiff to the defendants-respondents invalidates the provisions of 35 U.S.C. 102(c) and 35 U.S.C. 154.

2. Whether invention and monopoly of a product necessarily includes the making and the use of the product under 35 U.S.C. 101, 111, 112 and 154.

3. Whether 35 U.S.C. 251, 252 and 253 impose a duty on a patentee to correct errors in an issued patent or disclaim it.

Appendix E—Certificate of the Supreme Court of New Jersey

    4. Whether the Supremacy Clause, U.S. Const., Art. VI, requires that state courts apply the rules of the United States Patent Office in a field of federal pre-emption,

but the Supreme Court of New Jersey declines to certify that it passed upon any of these questions in deciding this case.

                    Joseph Weintraub, C.J.
       SUPREME COURT OF NEW JERSEY

Office-Supreme Court, U.S.
FILED

APR 1 11966

JOHN F. DAVIS, CLERK

IN THE

Supreme Court of the United States

OCTOBER TERM, 1965

Docket No. 595

739

FERNANDA MISANI,

Plaintiff-Appellant,

vs.

ORTHO PHARMACEUTICAL CORPORATION, a New
Jersey corporation, JOHNSON & JOHNSON, a New
Jersey corporation, ROBERT W. JOHNSON, HARRY
C. McKENZIE, BERTON J. TODD, EVAN R. SPALT,
JOHN FRIEBELY, and WILLIAM OROSHNIK,

Defendants-Appellees.

On Appeal from the Supreme Court of New Jersey

PETITION FOR REHEARING

FERNANDA MISANI,
Plaintiff-Appellant, pro se,
40 Tamaques Way,
Westfield, New Jersey.

TABLE OF CONTENTS

Cases Cited

IN THE

Supreme Court of the United States

OCTOBER TERM 1965

Docket No. 595

◆

FERNANDA MISANI,

Plaintiff-Appellant,

v.

ORTHO PHARMACEUTICAL CORPORATION,
a New Jersey Corporation, *et als.,*

Defendants-Appellees.

◆

Petition for Rehearing

Fernanda Misani, appellant, prays that this Court grant a rehearing of its Order of December 6, 1965, which dismissed the appeal for want of jurisdiction and treating the papers whereon the appeal was taken, as a petition for certiorari, denied certiorari.

In her petition for enlargement of the time within which to file the petition for rehearing, appellant urged that the two cases, *Brenner* v. *Manson,* —— U. S. ——, decided March 21, 1966, 34 U. S. Law Week 4221, and *Walker Process Equipment Inc.* v. *Food Machinery and Chemical Corporation,* 382 U. S. 172 (1965), involve issues identical to the present case. At the time of the petition for extension of time, no decision had been rendered in *Brenner v. Manson, supra,* and the *Walker* case had been unanimously reversed by this Court on December 6, 1965.

By Order of Justice Brennan, dated December 18, 1965, the time within which to file the petition for rehearing was extended for a period of twenty days beyond the decision of this Court in *Brenner* v. *Manson, supra.*

Certificate

I hereby certify that the foregoing petition for rehearing is presented in good faith and not for delay and is restricted to grounds specified in Rule 58(2) of the Rules of this Court, that is, to the issues decided by this Court in the intervening decision in *Brenner* v. *Manson,* —— U. S. —— (1966), 34 U. S. Law Week 4221, and the decision in *Walker Process Equipment Inc.* v. *Food Machinery and Chemical Corporation,* 382 U. S. 172 (1965) decided December 6, 1965.

FERNANDA MISANI

April 8, 1966

Reasons for Granting Rehearing, Noting Probable Jurisdiction, or Issuing the Writ

Subsequent to the Order of December 6, 1965, which dismissed the appeal and denied certiorari, this Court has passed on the identical issue of the requisites of patentability in *Brenner* v. *Manson*, —— U. S. —— (1966), 34 U. S. Law Week 4221. This intervening decision, which reversed the judgment below, is controlling. In *Brenner*, this Court, citing 35 U. S. C. 101, has held that no patent may be granted on a product, unless the product is shown to be useful:

> "The basic quid pro quo contemplated by the Constitution and the Congress for granting a patent monopoly is the benefit derived to the public from an invention with substantial utility."

The obvious corollary of this holding is that the inventor of a novel chemical compound is the individual who conceived the idea of making the compound, made it, and discovered the utility.

I. **The holding of the New Jersey Supreme Court that an individual may obtain a patent on a product, without a process for manufacturing the product and without a showing that the product has utility, is in conflict with the holding of this Court in *Brenner* v. *Manson*, —— U. S. —— (1966), 34 U. S. Law Week 4221 and invalidates 35 U. S. C. 101, 112 and 154.**

In the present case, a patent U.S.P. 2,878,263 (Jurisdictional Statement at p. 14*) issued in 1959, claiming the

---

* References in this petition are to the Jurisdictional Statement. Reply Brief in Opposition to Appellees' Motion to Dismiss the Appeal, and Appendixes A, B, C, D and E annexed thereto.

novel product 4-methyl 4-phenyl-5-pyrazolone. The patent describes in full detail the novel process of manufacture of the product and its novel properties in curing a serious disease, convulsions. The novel compound was the invention of the plaintiff, appellant herein, a senior chemist, the holder of a doctorate in Organic Chemistry, and with long experience in the particular field of this invention. The patent, however, designates Oroshnik, one of the defendants-appellees, as the inventor.

Oroshnik has alleged, with no proof whatsoever, that he merely conceived the idea of making the compound, but admits that he did not know how to manufacture the product, did not make it, and did not discover the novel use of the product. It is not disputed that the patent is based upon appellant's successful original scientific contribution and experimentation (Appendix C at 12a; Appendix B at 6a). Under the holding of this Court in *Brenner v. Manson, supra*, Oroshnik cannot be the inventor. Even assuming, for the sake of argument, that he conceived the idea of making the compound, a patentable invention requires the actual making of the compound and a showing of utility. The successful manufacture of the compound is, of course, a prerequisite before the compound may be tested, and the utility determined. U.S.P. 2,878,263 would not have issued in Oroshnik's name or anybody else's name, without the full description of the novel process for the manufacture of the substance and the novel properties of the substance as an anticonvulsant.

This action was brought for deprivation of intellectual credit, for the failure to designate the plaintiff as the inventor, and for fraud on the United States Patent Office for obtaining a patent with the false oath of one who was not the inventor.

According to the trial judge, no cause of action for deprivation of intellectual credit exists, and a scientist-employee, who has agreed to assign proprietary rights to the employer *"forfeits"* the right to have his or her name as the inventor in the patent (Jurisdictional Statement, at p. 7, 30). The Appellate Division of New Jersey reversed that monstrous and unconstitutional holding. That court properly held that a United States patent must be accompanied by the oath of the actual inventor, 35 U.S.C. 102(f); 35 U.S.C. 111; 35 U.S.C. 115; and that the right of inventorship is guaranteeed both by federal law and common law principles (Appendix C, 16a to 19a; Appendix D at 44). Further, the Appellate Division properly held that a patentable invention of a new compound requires, not only conception of the idea, but the making of the compound and a showing that it is useful (Appendix C, 19a).

The Supreme Court of New Jersey, however, has reversed the Appellate Division. It has held that the conception of idea of making a new compound, without the actual reduction to practice, and without the showing of utility, is sufficient for a patentable invention (Appendix B, 6a). The Supreme Court of New Jersey recognizes that the patent is based on appellant's scientific contribution, but relieves appellees from liability merely because *"the patent claim (one line) in U.S.P. 2,878,263 was carefully limited to the compound itself and did not extend to the process and use"* (Appendix B, at 7a; Jurisdictional Statement at 22 to 36). Thus, according to the Supreme Court of New Jersey, it is proper to obtain a patent on a new compound without the making of the compound and without a showing that the compound is useful. Further, according to the Supreme Court of New Jersey, it is proper for an employer to secure a patent in the name of one employee, merely because he alleges, without proof whatsoever, that he conceived the idea of making the compound, where the employer knows that another employee, not only conceived the idea, but successfully devised the means for making the compound and discovered the novel valuable use.

Thus, under the holding of the Supreme Court of New Jersey, an employer, in securing a patent in the name of one employee, may incorporate in the patent the successful experimentation of another employee, without which no patent would issue. It is submitted that the holding of the New Jersey Supreme Court ratifies a policy by the employer of deliberately obtaining patents with false oaths of one who is not the inventor, fraud on the United States Patent Office, and invalidation of federal law.

II. Under the holding of this Court in *Walker Process Equipment, Inc.* v. *Food Machinery and Chemical Corporation*, 382 U. S. 172 (1965), respondents-appellees have violated the antitrust laws, 15 U. S. C. 15, and should be liable for treble damages.

1. In the *Walker* case, this Court has unanimously held that delay in filing a patent application for more than one year after the invention has been exploited and introduced into public use, is a violation of 35 U.S.C. 102(b) and 102(c), and the inventor, or anyone claiming under him, forfeits the right to a monopoly on his invention. The fraud in the sworn allegations in the oath accompanying the application for the patent, makes the monopoly illegal and a violation of the antitrust laws. 15 U.S.C. 15. The injured party has a right to treble damages under the Clayton Antitrust Act.

The statutory provisions, 35 U.S.C. 102(b) and 102(c), pertain to loss of the right to a patent because of the delay in filing the application. In the present case, the same fraud and delay in filing undisputably exist. It is a fact that appellant, in December 1955, conceived the idea of making the substance described and claimed in U.S.P. 2,878,263, and in April, 1956, she successfully reduced the idea to practice, synthesized the substance by a novel process and discovered the valuable properties as an anticonvulsant. She was maliciously discharged three days later. It has not been contested that Johnson & Johnson's legal staff, in April 1956, prepared the patent application based on appellant's invention but did not file it in the United States Patent Office until two years later, February 1958 (Jurisdictional Statement, at p. 33). Appellees' delay in filing the patent application is identical to the *Walker* case, *supra*, and constitutes an illegal monopoly. 15 U.S.C. 15. The reason for the delay, according to their own admissions, was suppression of the invention and concealment, for malicious motives.

Our patent laws require that the inventor or anyone claiming under him, must content himself with either secrecy or legal monopoly. He must act with speed and diligence in filing the application for a patent or his rights to a legal monopoly are forever barred. The condition for securing a patent is giving the public the fruits of the invention as soon as possible, and preventing concealment and abandonment. This object was set forth in *Pennock* v. *Dialogue*, 27 U. S. 2 (Pet) 1, 19 (1829); *Woodbridge* v. *United States,* 263 U. S. 50 (1923); *Kendall* v. *Winsor,* 62 U. S. 322 (1858); *Motion Picture Patents Co.* v. *Universal Film Mfg. Co.,* 243 U. S. 502 (1917). The same rationale is at the basis of this Court's decision in *Walker.*

The New Jersey courts have reached a result totally conflicting with our antitrust and patent laws, 15 U. S. C. 15, 35 U. S. C. 102(b) and 102(c), and the *Walker* holding of this Court. They have expressly held that an employer has a legal right to delay in filing applications for patents, conceal invention of employees, abandon them, *"throw them out of the window", "scrap"* them and long time after, secure patent rights at its *"unfettered will"* (Appendix B at 3a; Appendix C at 14a; Jurisdictional Statement at 33-34). The statutory duty of promptly filing the application for a patent does not apply to the employer. It is submitted that the holding of the New Jersey courts is a ratification of an illegal monopoly and must be reversed.

2. In *Walker Process Equipment Inc. v. Food Machinery and Chemical Corporation,* this Court has said that an assignee, who maintains and enforces a patent with knowledge of its infirmity, violates the antitrust laws. 15 U. S. C. 15. Under this holding, appellees have violated the antitrust laws and appellant is entitled to treble damages.

Johnson & Johnson before the New Jersey courts and as late as their brief in support of their motion to dismiss the appeal before this Court, has argued that U.S.P. 2,878,263 is invalid (Appellees' brief at 4, 7, 9, 10; Appendix B at 5a; Appendix C at 13a, 18a), but has retained and maintained the illegal monopoly, and has refused to disclaim it. 35 U. S. C. 253. The refusal to disclaim has been deliberate. Before the New Jersey courts, Johnson & Johnson has said:

> "We could disclaim, but that is solely within our privilege to do so or not to do so, we are the owners of the patent." (Jurisdictional Statement at p. 36)

Also Food Machinery and Chemical Corporation in *Walker, supra,* was the owner of the patent. Yet, in a belated, but at least good faith gesture, it moved to withdraw its complaint and has forfeited the right to a monopoly. In direct contrast, the New Jersey courts have ratified the arbitrary power of the employer to retain an illegal monopoly and violation of our antitrust laws. They have said:

"She has no right to say [that they should disclaim it] ... that is their business, that is not her business. ... If they want [to disclaim it] they can do it, and if they don't want to, they don't have to do it and she has no rights on that." (Appendix C at 15a; Jurisdictional Statement at 37)

Thus, the New Jersey courts, in clear conflict with the holding in *Walker*, permit an employer to retain and enforce an invalid patent, and simultaneously deny damages to the injured employee.

3. Unless the conflict between *Walker* and the present case is eliminated, the dismissal of the appeal amounts to an illegal discrimination against the large class of scientists, the employed inventors, and in favor of the employers. This discrimination is against the very class of individuals, who, by their initiative and inventive ability, coupled with extensive academic training, are credited with giving our country its superior technological position. They are the thousands of individuals whom the Constitution, U. S. Const., Art. 1, Sec. 8, Cl. 8, and our patent laws, are designed to protect.

In *Walker*, this Court has distinguished between the actual fraud, the willful and deliberate submission of a false oath and the honest errors, which are classified as technical fraud, for which this Court relieves the patentee from liability. Application of this rule to the present case, undisputably leads to a reversal, just as in *Walker*. Johnson & Johnson knew and has admitted that Oroshnik was not the inventor, and knew that they would have lost the interference proceeding before the Board of Interferences in the United States Patent Office (Jurisdictional Statement at pp. 11-13, 29). This is not an honest error, but actual knowledge that Oroshnik was not the inventor and that the sworn allegation by Oroshnik in the application which issued as U.S.P. 2,878,263, was false and a fraud upon the United States Patent Office.

III. This Court has jurisdiction of this appeal.

The dismissal of this appeal for want of jurisdiction, as stated in the Order of December 6, 1965, implies that according to this Court, the federal questions were not raised below or that the New Jersey courts have, neither expressly nor impliedly, passed on the validity of federal statutes. The Court is respectfully urged to reconsider this ground of dismissal.

The Supreme Court of New Jersey has certified that the federal questions were timely and properly argued below (Appendix E, appended to appellant's reply brief), has not attempted to rest its decision on an independent non-federal ground, and has cited 35 U. S. C. 112 (Appendix B, at 6a). The Supreme Court of New Jersey, however, in passing upon the federal questions, has essentially invalidated federal law.

CONCLUSION

It is respectfully urged that rehearing be granted and probable jurisdiction be noted or a writ of certiorari issue to the Supreme Court of New Jersey.

Unless the order of dismissal of the appeal is reversed, the disposition below of this case is in sharp conflict with the decision of this Court in *Walker Process Equipment Inc.* v. *Food Machinery and Chemical Corporation*, 382 U. S. 172 (1965), and *Brenner* v. *Manson*, U. S. (1966), 34 U. S. Law Week 4221.

An employer, according to the New Jersey courts, has no duty to file patent applications promptly, is free to "*scrap*" inventions of employees and long time afterwards, s permitted to secure patent rights. An employer may obtain patents with false oaths by one who is not the inventor, has no duty to disclaim an invalid patent and is permitted to prolong the monopoly beyond the seventeen-year period (Jurisdictional Statement, at page 22).

According to the New Jersey courts, the employee-inventor has no right to have his or her name on a patent, and is not permitted to prove the extent of damages for the delay in filing the patent application and for the willful and malicious concealment of his or her inventions.

Respectfully submitted,

FERNANDA MISANI,
Appellant-Petitioner, pro se.